About this book

This experienced writer on human rights explores the relationship between economic globalization and human rights. Koen De Feyter, who has chaired Amnesty International's Working Group on economic, social and cultural rights, shows the many ways in which rampant market economics in today's world leads to violations of human rights. He questions how far the present-day international human rights system – focusing as it does on legal conventions and enforcement by state machinery – really provides effective protection against the adverse effects of globalization.

He makes positive and innovative suggestions for improving the human rights system – including:

- Rethinking the state's obligations in a context where it may no longer be directly responsible for providing a service that is essential to the realization of a particular right;
- Creating human rights responsibilities for other actors than the state – notably big companies and international financial institutions like the World Bank.
- Developing human rights obligations on the part of states beyond their own national territories.

This accessible and thought-provoking book explains globalization to human rights activists as well as the relevance of a human rights approach in combating the downsides of globalization. In doing so, it shows both human rights activists and participants in the anti-globalization and development movements that there is a large, but hitherto untapped, overlap in their agendas, and real potential for a strategic alliance between them in joint campaigns around issues they share.

D0209164

About the author

Koen De Feyter has taught and researched on human rights and development issues for twenty years. He has done fieldwork for both non-governmental and governmental actors. He has observed trials in Northern Ireland and elections in Burundi. He was part of a commission of inquiry into massive killings in a refugee camp in Rwanda, and worked with a Philippine human rights organization on forced evictions, and in Brazil on agrarian reform. He has contributed to the work of Amnesty International in a number of capacities, including as chair of an advisory committee to its international board on the development of the human rights movement in the South, and as chair of its working group on economic, social and cultural rights

In 2004–2005, he coordinated the European Master in Human Rights and Democratization programme in Venice. His permanent affiliation is both with the Institute of Development Policy and Management, University of Antwerp and at the Centre for Human Rights, University of Maastricht.

His publications include the books *Privatisation and Human Rights* (2005) (co-edited with Felipe Gomez) and *World Development Law* (2001) (both published in Antwerp by Intersentia), and various articles on human rights and development law.

KOEN DE FEYTER

Human rights

Social justice in the age of the market

University Press
DHAKA

White Lotus
BANGKOK

Fernwood Publishing
NOVA SCOTIA

Books for Change
BANGALORE

SIRD
KUALA LUMPUR

David Philip
CAPE TOWN

Zed Books
LONDON | NEW YORK

Human rights: Social justice in the age of the market was first published in 2005, by:

in Bangladesh: The University Press Ltd, Red Crescent Building, 114 Motijheel C/A, PO Box 2611, Dhaka 1000

in Burma, Cambodia, Laos, Thailand and Vietnam: White Lotus Co. Ltd, GPO Box 1141, Bangkok 10501, Thailand

in Canada: Fernwood, 8422 St Margaret's Bay Road (Hwy 3), Site 2A, Box 5, Black Point, Nova Scotia BOJ 1BO

in India: Books for Change, 139 Richmond Road, Bangalore 560 025

in Malaysia: Strategic Information Research Department (SIRD), No. 11/4E, Petaling Jaya, 46200 Selangor

in Southern Africa: David Philip Publishers (Pty Ltd), 99 Garfield Road, Claremont 7700, South Africa

in the rest of the world: Zed Books Ltd, 7 Cynthia Street, London N1 9JF, UK and Room 400, 175 Fifth Avenue, New York, NY 10010, USA

www.zedbooks.co.uk

Cover designed by Andrew Corbett
Set in Arnhem and Futura Bold by Ewan Smith, London
Printed and bound in the EU by Cox and Wyman, Reading

Distributed in the USA exclusively by Palgrave Macmillan, a division of St Martin's Press, LLC, 175 Fifth Avenue, New York, NY 10010.

A catalogue record for this book is available from the British Library
US CIP data are available from the Library of Congress

Library and Archives Canada Cataloguing in Publication
Feyter, K. de (Koen)
    Human rights : social justice in the age of the market / Koen de Feyter.
(Global issues series)
Includes bibliographical references and index.
ISBN 1-55266-167-9

    1. Civil rights. 2. Human rights. 3. Globalization.
I. Title. II. Series: Global issues (Halifax, N.S.)
JC571.F485 2005a   323   C2005-901463-6

ISBN 1 55266 167 9 (Canada)
ISBN 81 8291 015 3 (India)
ISBN 983 2535 62 X (Malaysia)
ISBN 1 84277 486 7 hb (rest of the world)
ISBN 1 84277 487 5 pb

A Brave New Series

GLOBAL ISSUES
IN A CHANGING WORLD

This new series of short, accessible think-pieces deals with leading global issues of relevance to humanity today. Intended for the enquiring reader and social activists in the North and the South, as well as students, the books explain what is at stake and question conventional ideas and policies. Drawn from many different parts of the world, the series' authors pay particular attention to the needs and interests of ordinary people, whether living in the rich industrial or the developing countries. They all share a common objective: to help stimulate new thinking and social action in the opening years of the new century.

Global Issues in a Changing World is a joint initiative by Zed Books in collaboration with a number of partner publishers and non-governmental organizations around the world. By working together, we intend to maximize the relevance and availability of the books published in the series.

Participating NGOs

Both ENDS, Amsterdam
Catholic Institute for International Relations, London
Corner House, Sturminster Newton
Council on International and Public Affairs, New York
Dag Hammarskjöld Foundation, Uppsala
Development GAP, Washington DC
Focus on the Global South, Bangkok
IBON: Manila
Inter Pares, Ottawa
Public Interest Research Centre, Delhi
Third World Network, Penang
Third World Network–Africa, Accra
World Development Movement, London

About this series

Communities in the South are facing great difficulties in coping with global trends. I hope this brave new series will throw much-needed light on the issues ahead and help us choose the right options.

Martin Khor, Director, Third World Network, Penang

There is no more important campaign than our struggle to bring the global economy under democratic control. But the issues are fearsomely complex. This Global Issues series is a valuable resource for the committed campaigner and the educated citizen.

Barry Coates, Director, Oxfam New Zealand

Zed Books has long provided an inspiring list about the issues that touch and change people's lives. The Global Issues series is another dimension of Zed's fine record, allowing access to a range of subjects and authors that, to my knowledge, very few publishers have tried. I strongly recommend these new, powerful titles and this exciting series.

John Pilger, author

We are all part of a generation that actually has the means to eliminate extreme poverty worldwide. Our task is to harness the forces of globalization for the benefit of working people, their families and their communities – that is our collective duty. The Global Issues series makes a powerful contribution to the global campaign for justice, sustainable and equitable development, and peaceful progress.

Glenys Kinnock MEP

Contents

Boxes and figure

Boxes

Figure

Acknowledgements

Here are the names of some people I am grateful to: Heidy Rombouts, for allowing me to use her field research on victim organizations in Rwanda before its publication (at the end of Chapter 3); Marije Mellegers at the University of Maastricht for collecting materials in support of the 9/11 chapter; Antenor Hallo De Wolf, also at the University of Maastricht, for sharing his files on the response of the Geneva human rights system to privatization issues (Chapter 5); Caroline Lopes of the European Master on Human Rights and Democratization for translating the MST poem that appears in Box 5.9; Simone Longo de Andrade from the same Master for giving me permission to use an excerpt from her thesis in Chapter 7; the participants at the 2002 Maastricht conference on agrarian reform and human rights, and at the 2004 Venice conference on privatization and human rights for the ideas they offered; and Robert Molteno at Zed for all. Responsibility for the text is my own.

1 | Introduction

Human rights mean different things to different people. While I was writing this book in Belgium, two advertising campaigns promoted *Freedom of Speech!* A mobile phone provider put up billboards along the motorways using the slogan in an attempt to break into a market long dominated by a public operator. A political party of the extreme right launched the second campaign, in an attack on a Court judgment which had condemned organizations associated with it for violations of the law on racism. The party won in the subsequent elections.

This book is not about how human rights can serve the interests of a company or of a racist party. It investigates whether human rights can assist people abandoned by globalization in achieving human dignity.

It is not self-evident that human rights can offer protection in a globalized world. International human rights law developed at a time when states monopolized international relations. The international human rights system was similarly state-orientated. Domestic states carried human rights obligations *vis-à-vis* their inhabitants, but not *vis-à-vis* anyone else. The entire system relied on connecting every individual to a responsible state that had the capacity to deliver protection. Other actors, such as companies or international economic organizations, remained out of sight.

In today's globalized world, however, human rights violations often occur as a consequence of the behaviour of a variety of actors. Consider: a fifteen-year old girl, who leaves her own country because she cannot provide for herself or her family, is enlisted in prostitution by a trafficking ring in the country she travels to, is maltreated during a police raid as a prelude to a forcible return to her home country, where the cycle starts all over again. The girl cannot achieve a dignified life because of the cumulative effect of the actions of her home state, the traffickers, and of the country of destination. In order for human rights protection to work, an integrated global response that challenges the behaviour of all perpetrators, and interacts with each of them, is necessary. Focusing on only one actor often brings no improvement at all. Human rights need to adjust to the context of globalization, in much the same way they adjusted earlier to the Holocaust, or to the Iron Curtain. This book approaches human rights as a living instrument, not as texts set in stone.

If time is of the essence, read Chapter 2. Its objective is to contribute to the development of a theory of human rights that responds to the challenges of globalization. Proposed directions for human rights follow a brief review of the different dimensions of globalization.

It is argued that existing state obligations in the field of human rights need to be rethought. Consider: a state decides to privatize the water supply system of its major cities. The privatization does not diminish the state's obligation to provide poor people with access to drinking water. What does change, however, is what the state needs to do in order to guarantee access. The roles of provider and supervisor are different, and this affects the legal techniques through which protection must be ensured. It is essential that the human rights project clarifies what human rights require from the state in these changed circumstances.

Second, in a globalized world, the human rights obligations of states are simply not enough. Mechanisms need to be created that ensure the accountability of *other actors* for human rights. These actors include influential economic powers whose actions drive people into poverty. The World Trade Organization and the International Monetary Fund should not be able to declare human rights irrelevant to their work. Companies should not take

2

cover behind the profit motive in order to absolve themselves of responsibility for human rights violations in which they are complicit.

Finally, if human rights are to make a difference, they should focus on empowering those who suffer the worst abuse. The experience of people alienated by the globalization process should inform the direction of the human rights project, rather than the extent to which dominant actors are willing to accommodate aspects of human rights that serve their interests.

Chapters 3 to 5 provide a reality check. Is there any hope that the human rights project will move in the proposed direction? The obstacles are formidable.

Current human rights law shares some of the general weaknesses of international law. The enforcement of compliance is not its greatest strength. Although considerable progress has been achieved over the last fifty years, success remains dependent on the political will of (powerful) governmental and private actors. Governments use the human rights discourse selectively to achieve foreign policy goals, and the legitimacy of human rights as cosmopolitan values shared by all humanity suffers accordingly. Relationships of interdependence apply to the global human rights system in much the same way as they do to other fields of international relations. The relative capacities of actors perpetrating violations and of those requiring justice determine outcomes. In addition, some human rights proponents oppose reform, primarily out of fear for the loss of what has been gained. Torture remains torture, whether the world is globalizing or not, and there is a risk that the acknowledgement of the responsibility of non-state actors makes it easier for states to escape. Why not close one's eyes to the causes of violations, and stick to documenting abuse and demanding justice in each individual case? Human rights advocates may find comfort in the familiarity of the case file approach.

3

The 11 September 2001 attacks left their mark on human rights, as they did on everything else. The attacks were carefully planned to achieve the highest possible loss of life, and were committed for political gain. They share these characteristics with a number of gross and systematic violations perpetrated by states in the past. In response, anti-terrorism measures went beyond permissible limitations of civil and political rights. War was deemed just even if international law held that it was illegal. International donors discovered a new priority: the strengthening of the capacity of security systems in the perceived countries of origin of terrorists, notwithstanding the dubious human rights reputation of recipient regimes. This book is primarily concerned with economic globalization and its impact on human rights. Nevertheless, many of the proposals on human rights reform in Chapter 2 are also relevant to a human rights response to 11 September and its aftermath.

Consider the global nature of the events: a transnational non-state network perpetrated the attacks. The attacks were arguably planned in one country and executed in another. Private security firms were involved in interrogation practices in the Abu Ghraib prison. The United States held suspected terrorists in secret detention centres in various countries.

None of these practices fits well in an approach that thinks only in terms of the responsibility of a state for what happens on its own territory. But the need to ensure the human rights of the people affected by the different events is no less urgent. Again, new tools are needed to protect the same values in a changed context.

It would be unfair to list the UN Geneva human rights system as an obstacle to human rights protection. The UN chapter takes its rightful place between the chapters on obstacles and on opportunities. The Geneva system inspires feelings of both hope and despair. Much depends on how one evaluates success. One

4

may take the view that a single life saved because of an urgent action by a Geneva Special Rapporteur makes it worthwhile to maintain the institution. Or five lives. Or ten. This is a respectable position. If the test is, however, whether the Geneva system fulfils the role of a global forum capable of translating the experience of those who suffer grave abuse at the local level into effective but sufficiently flexible global norms and action, the system fails. Globalization has not strengthened the UN Geneva human rights institutions. They are arguably less effective now than they were during the Cold War. Certainly, the Geneva human rights regime has been unable so far to deal in a meaningful way with post-Cold War challenges, such as the impact of the business world and the international economic organizations that drive globalization, on the rights the institutions are deemed to protect.

Chapters 6 and 7 take a more optimistic view of the proposals in the second chapter. Chapter 6 looks at developments in human rights that go in the right direction. Progress in holding companies accountable is mapped. The willingness of the World Bank to allow a degree of direct accountability to people adversely affected by Bank-supported projects is discussed. Latin American and African regional protection systems have responded in an encouraging way to violations affecting entire communities. The decisions build on the different legal traditions of these continents, and thus introduce a welcome element of plurality in the human rights discourse. The chapter opens with a discussion of peoples' tribunals, i.e. public opinion tribunals set up by NGOs to demonstrate that a legal approach building directly on the experiences of those suffering abuse is possible. There is a conscious effort in the chapter to start from the bottom up, by looking at the usefulness of the different procedural devices from the perspective of organizations working for the defence of human rights.

Chapter 7 applies the preferred human rights approach to

5

several aspects of economic globalization. The aim is to demonstrate how the efficacy of human rights in offering protection in these situations can be improved. But also, and perhaps more importantly, to show the added value of a human rights approach as compared to the current, standard approaches that are predominantly determined by an economic analysis. The chapter reviews agrarian reform, the impact of intellectual property rights on health, the privatization of services, and the provision of micro-credit to people living in extreme poverty. Many a human rights advocate may at first sight not recognize these issues as human rights related. References to human rights may well be absent from international regulation on these issues, thus obscuring the link to human rights. As the chapter seeks to demonstrate, this in no way prevents the relevant rules and practices from having an impact on human rights, nor does it mean that human rights have nothing to contribute to the issues. On the contrary, it is precisely the conscious separation of human rights from these agreements, rules and practices that causes human rights harm.

All of the above leads to a final finding. An urgent need exists for the human rights movement and the movement favouring alternative forms of globalization to pool resources. An open mind on both sides is required, and a willingness to abandon the cocoon of acquired wisdom. Only if there is cross-fertilization between the ideas of both movements, and between the different disciplines that support their vision (development economics, law, social sciences, international relations), can a strong alternative to the current blend of economic globalization be developed.

2 | Essentials

Imagine there's no political or social constraint on markets. National economic barriers have collapsed, and a global economy has emerged where private actors compete for the accumulation of wealth, unhindered by spatial or social boundaries. International organizations have laid down rules that constrain states from using sovereign power to interfere with market objectives. Individuals are consumers, and they consume, optimally. Lifestyles converge, and a global culture gradually erases divisive cultural differences. It's easy if you try.

But it hasn't happened yet. Globalization essentially is 'a particular way of organizing social life across existing State borders' (Sklair 2002: 8). *Economic* globalization consists of the breaking down of state borders in order to allow the free flow of finance, trade, production and labour. Writers of various ideological persuasions agree that this process of liberalization is incomplete: far advanced in the field of finance, but very modest in the area of labour. The global world evoked above does not yet exist.

Dimensions of globalization

Since the 1970s, removal of capital controls by major developed countries has resulted in a significant increase in trade in foreign exchange. Freedom of capital movement resulted in the integration of domestic capital markets; it also enabled developing countries to access capital that was not available internally. Foreign exchange transactions are, however, notoriously speculative and often short-term, making countries vulnerable to sudden shifts in financial flows, as demonstrated by the financial crises in Mexico and South-East Asia in the 1990s. There is no international regime regulating international finance. Calls have been made to introduce international controls, particularly on short-term capital (cf. Gilpin 2001: 271–7), or, in the absence of such international controls, to allow countries the flexibility to retain or reintroduce capital controls domestically (Khor 2001: 68–71).

The succession of the GATT system by the World Trade Organization (WTO) clearly increased the range of trade liberalization, if only because the scope of application of the WTO treaties reached beyond the trade in goods, and included areas such as trade in services and the protection of intellectual property rights. Developed countries wish to bringing additional areas within the WTO remit. The WTO dispute settlement system includes incentives for compliance that are unusually strong in international law. Once states undertake commitments in the WTO context, they are difficult to reverse. On the other hand, developed countries still protect trade in vital areas such as agriculture, textiles and a number of manufactured goods (e.g. cars). Developing countries wish to maintain barriers in areas such as services, in an attempt to safeguard autonomy from foreign providers in fields that impact directly on policies with major development implications.

Foreign direct investment (FDI) involves a long-term relationship and a lasting interest and control by a resident enterprise of one country (the foreign direct investor or the parent country) in an enterprise resident in another country. Negotiations during the 1990s over a multilateral investment agreement that would have greatly enhanced the rights of international investors *vis-à-vis* host countries failed, but significant increases in FDI nevertheless occurred as a consequence of liberalization measures decided at the national and bilateral levels. The UNCTAD *World Investment Report 2002* notes that, in 2001, seventy-one countries made 208 changes in FDI laws, more than 90 per cent of which were aimed at making the investment climate more favourable to inward FDI. UNCTAD counted 2,099 bilateral investment treaties by the end of 2001. The report confirms that transnational corporations (TNCs) still expand their role in the world economy. Foreign affiliates accounted for about 54 million employees in 2001, compared to 24 million in 1990. Nevertheless, major regional differences remain in actual FDI flows. The African continent attracted a mere 2 per cent of global FDI inflows in 2001.

Finally, at least in liberal economic theory, economic openness should also apply to the movement of labour. Workers should be able to move to where they are most productive: 'the case for unrestricted labour mobility is as compelling as the case for unrestricted capital mobility or the case for free trade' (Nayyar 2002b: 166). As in the area of foreign direct investment, there is no international regime liberalizing cross-border movement, but, differently, liberalization does not result from domestic immigration laws or consular practices either. States invoke both security concerns and, ironically, territorially confined duties of distributive justice to resist liberalizing the movement of labour. The mix of the rationale of economic globalization that pushes individuals to seek work opportunities across borders with huge domestic barriers to entry creates significant irregular migration (Jordan and Düvell 2002). Like others, Bhagwati perceives international migration to be unstoppable. Rather than bemoaning the brain-drain, his prescription to developing countries is to accept a diaspora model, integrating present and past citizens into a web of rights and obligations in the extended community defined with the home country as the centre. Less imaginatively, his advice to developed countries is to integrate migrants into their new homes in ways that will minimize the social costs and maximize economic benefits (Bhagwati 2003). Interestingly, Stark argues that even if 'migration leakage' occurs, developing countries still benefit from allowing controlled emigration, because the prospect of migration induces people to invest more

9

in education: 'Higher prospective returns to human capital in a foreign country impinge on human capital formation decisions at home' (Stark 2004). At the end of the day, only some will be able to migrate, while others will remain in their society with better skills.

The cultural dimension of globalization attracts attention as well. Sklair explains how economic globalization depends on the promotion by corporate actors of the culture-ideology of consumerism, a project that aims at persuading people 'to consume not simply to satisfy their biological and other modest needs but in response to artificially created desires' (Sklair 2002: 62). There is no real hope, however, that these desires can be satisfied in the foreseeable future, particularly in the South.

Box 2.1 *'US Babies Get Global Brand Names'*

Americans are increasingly turning to the world of popular culture to name their children, a study has found. Children have been named after big brands as diverse as beauty company L'Oreal, car firm Chevrolet and designer clothes company Armani [...] Mr Evans, a professor at Bellevue University, Nebraska, has studied baby names in the US for 25 years [...] Mr Evans told BBC News Online one reason for the popularity of brands as names is a growing desire on the part of parents to mark their children out as different. He also says that naming a child after a brand such as Armani or Chanel, associated with money or exclusivity, reflects the material hopes of such families. 'It is no different from the 19th century when parents named their children Ruby or Opal ... it reflects their aspirations', he says.

Source: BBC News Online, 13 November 2003

In the context of this process, instruments of homogenization (Appadurai 1999: 229) are used, such as advertising, the propagation of lifestyles or of English as a global language. These instruments are used by Westerners, but also by social groups that associate with economic globalization in non-Western societies. Together, these groups form alliances that escape state sovereignty. Societies differ in how they absorb such pressures: there may be assimilation, but also confrontation or closure. Often different trends occur simultaneously, making the management of cultural differences within societies a fundamental problem of contemporary political systems (Cesari 2002: 17).

States, markets etc.

Globalization affects the capacity of the state to exercise sovereignty over its territory. International law confers sovereign rights on the population of a state, which the government exercises on its behalf. According to the law, the government freely decides both domestic and foreign policy. As a consequence of globalization these decisions are, in fact and to some extent in law, affected by external actors. They include not only companies and organizations that operate across borders, but also other influential states.

States and market forces Clearly, companies that organize across borders define the primary role of a state in terms of creating a space for the play of market forces. Not only should a state adopt a market-based system within its own territory (and thus engage in policies of deregulation and privatization if previously the state had directly intervened in the economy), the same system should apply to economic relationships *among* countries. Within each state, firms participating in the global economy constitute an important domestic political influence that governments cannot easily ignore. There may not be many incentives for resisting

Essentials

the corporate agenda if both the politics and the economy of a country are elitist in nature. In addition, transnational companies are themselves international networks that coordinate action: TNCs thus have the capacity to influence a state's policy both from within and from above.

Nevertheless, even states that take a positive view of economic globalization may not fully share the globalist corporate view. The state's main responsibility is to the population in its own territory, and not to the world community. Similarly, the state's primary interest is in the national economy. States may well refuse the unfettered play of market forces if the result is beneficial for the world economy, but damages the territorial economy, including the interests of local firms. Unlike some companies, governments do not have the option of displacing their activities to another territory. Nor are they able to ignore accountability to the population.

Against this background, it comes as no surprise that one current in the counter-movement to economic globalization is not about promoting alternative global values, but about preserving national or religious identity. In an interesting study of right-wing nationalism in the United States, Rupert describes how adherents to the theory perceive economic globalization as a threat to the special (individualistic, Christian, white) identity of America. In this analysis, the US government does far too little to protect the interests of the American middle class. Its agenda should be set in response to the needs of Mr Smith and Mr Deeds, not in response to the Wall Street financial elite and transnational corporations (Rupert 2000: 94–118). Radical Islamism, which emerged as a strong counter-force to economic globalization in the 1990s, also takes as its point of departure the need to defend the identity of the community of believers and the superior values embedded in Islam.

Does the theory of economic globalization allow any role for the social responsibility of the state? The notion of 'market failures' opens up a role for state intervention when markets fail to produce the desired outcomes. The theory applies, for instance, when a firm's economic activity creates external costs borne by the population at large, but not by the individual producer, creating room for state intervention in the area of environmental protection. Another traditionally recognized market failure is inadequate consumer information, preventing the consumer from making optimal choices. Whether the concept also covers distributive inequality, however, is controversial. In any case, the rationale for intervening is an economic one, and is not based on the recognition of the inherent value of either the environment or of democratic process. In a similar vein, the concept of 'public goods' refers to goods that are of little interest to private operators because they cannot easily be sold. Clean air is often cited as an example. It is to the benefit of all that the air is clean, but all breathe the air on the street at no cost. Hence, the need for a non-market actor to provide the common good. UNDP has promoted a theory of global public goods, extending the application of the concept to such fields as peace and security, education, health and equity and justice (Kaul et al. 2003).

It has been argued that the pursuit of social justice will remain a function of the state, if only in order to legitimize the functioning of the market. Market mechanisms are by nature exclusive in rewarding performers only, and thus tend to create growing inequality. The vocation of the state, however, is to be inclusive. In order to protect the market, and also its own legitimacy, the state needs to intervene when marginalization occurs (Bhaduri 2002: 40). National political authorities 'will retain a unique advantage in justifying extractions for redistributive purposes' (McGinnis 2000: 56). States still have the freedom to pursue human development. Nevertheless, there appears to be a consensus that economic globalization encourages states to downsize social welfare spending, and to give priority to balancing budgets and avoiding high taxation rates (Prakash and Hart 2000: 13–16).

There are also instances when economic globalization increases gender inequality, as when the introduction of new technology to men in sectors previously controlled by women brings about a loss of women's control over income. Liberalization processes in the EU's new member-states do not appear to have a positive impact on gender pay gaps. Realization of the UN 2000 Millennium Development Goal 'to promote gender equality and the empowerment of women as effective ways to combat poverty, hunger and disease and to stimulate development that is truly sustainable' is a long way off. On the other hand, early analysis of the effect on the employment of women by TNCs in export processing zones, depicting such employment as contributing to oppression, has made way for studies pointing out that such employment may also lead to more social autonomy and women organizing against injustice in the workplace (Athreya 2002: 342–6). Perhaps the main finding is that, regardless of whether the effects on gender inequality are positive or negative in a specific case, states appear to accept them. In taking decisions on globalization, states do not prioritize its impact on gender inequality.

It is as if both states and TNCs suffer from an identity crisis. States introduce management styles copied from private actors, while TNCs insist that they are not about profit only, but about people and the planet as well. States switch from public consultation to cost–benefit analysis as a basis for decision-making (Aman 2000: 267). Corporate actors invest in transparency, and in public reporting on their contribution to sustainable development. In international development aid, public–private partnerships are the order of the day.

In conclusion, a reasonable approach appears to be that if economic globalization is the dominant policy prescription, both markets and states may fail in producing *ecological sustainability* and *social justice*, if only because neither is a direct objective of a global market system, or, as Sklair argues, they belong to a competing concept of globalization (Sklair 2002: 48–57). Therefore, as a minimum, 'correcting devices' (Khor 2001: 124) against both state and market deficiencies need to be provided for, in order to ensure the adjustment of economic rationales to environmental and social goals. It is unlikely that in the absence of such correctives major progress in human development for people purposely excluded by markets and abandoned by states will occur.

States and international organizations A number of intergovernmental organizations facilitate economic globalization through the establishment of rules that permit, prescribe or prohibit state action. National policy-making increasingly comes under the activities of these organizations.

The clearest examples are the loan conditionalities set by the international financial institutions (IFIs). Such conditionalities are an instrument through which states are obliged to open up to the global economy and to introduce or deepen domestic market systems. States that depend heavily on external funding, and particularly those that are heavily indebted, have little bargaining power and little real choice but to acquiesce in IFI remedies (Darrow 2003: 56–61). In Africa, the high level of external intervention in policy decisions has meant that African states are more accountable to foreign creditor nations and international institutions than to their own people (Cheru 2002: 20). The direct impact of IFIs on the living conditions of people (and in the World Bank's case, its presence in the field) has led to increasing calls for the establishment of direct accountability of the IFIs to local populations (Khor 2001: 121).

The World Trade Organization offers a very different example. According to Gilpin, the WTO has more authority over national policies than any other international economic organization, particularly because its judicial and regulatory powers extend to the major industrialized powers. The WTO 'approaches the neo-liberal institutionalist ideal of an effective supranational institution' (Gilpin 2001: 382). On the other hand, Lake points out that the WTO does not really create greater global governance. The organization has no higher authorities to which the members transfer power, only a dispute settlement system that aims at ensuring compliance with rules that are primarily designed to constrain states and limit their policy options. In reality, WTO rules expand the private sphere in which companies can operate. In Lake's view, 'globalization and global governance may well stand opposed to one another' (Lake 2000: 46–8).

Clearly, the WTO is a contested organization, because deep disagreement remains about whether its purpose, and the purpose of the international economy as a whole, should simply be to promote unrestricted free trade and open markets. Many would question whether the functioning of the organization has brought us any closer to the self-proclaimed goals of raising standards of living and the optimal use of the world's resources in accordance with the objective of sustainable development. A different view of the WTO as an international organization – in keeping with the realist view of international organizations – is as a stage where contending views of globalization do battle, in conference halls and green rooms, and on the streets.

The above does not imply that international organizations by necessity need to serve the purpose of promoting economic globalization. They could just as well be used as a vehicle for the realization of non-market objectives, e.g. as mechanisms for redistributing the benefits of economic globalization to the poor. Hopes were held at one time that the United Nations' development organizations would fulfil such a role. Many writers on globalization identify 'missing institutions' at the global level, including for the organization of cross-border movement, the governance of corporations, the provision of global public goods and the regulation of global public bads (Nayyar 2002c). Walden Bello remains sceptical, arguing for instance that a new UN Economic Security Council would 'simply translate into a centralization of rich country control over the global economy' (Bello 2002: 92). His preference is for the strengthening of regional economic blocs, at least if they can be construed in a non-elitist way. Ideally, in Bello's view, a central role of international organizations would be to express and protect local and national cultures by embodying and sheltering their distinctive practices (ibid., p. 118).

International organizations also include international non-governmental organizations (NGOs). Open borders benefit TNCs, but also global networking by NGOs. International NGOs fulfil a wide variety of roles. As providers of essential services, they may, like companies, provide functions that were once part of state responsibilities. Questions about how private operators are accountable to affected populations apply both to TNCs and NGOs operating across borders.

International NGOs are closer to IGOs when their aim is to influence decision-making by states or other actors. Advocacy NGOs defend a variety of causes, including the cause of economic globalization, but arguably their strongest impact has been on issues such as development, the environment and human rights. Compared to states, international NGOs are, potentially at least, not tied to a territorial/national interest perspective, and able to concentrate on the global value they seek to defend. Often, but not necessarily, the perspective of non-dominant political groups informs their positions (De Feyter 2001a: 219). Globalization has facilitated NGO networking across borders, and also influences the work of local NGOs. In a study of Indian gender-based NGOs, Singh finds that local NGOs started adopting global terms (such

17

as 'violence against women') that facilitate linking up with international campaigns, at the same time when India opened up its economy (Singh 2001: 115). Others point out that local NGOs run the risk of becoming 'internally elitist and externally servile to overseas donors' when they link up globally (Petras and Veltmeyer 2001: 132).

States and other states By definition, economically dominant states have more capacity to influence the economic policies of other states. Globalization unlocks additional channels of influence. As explained above, the policies of economically dominant states are not simply pro economic globalization. Security concerns and the interests of specific domestic markets also inform them. As a result, the global economy, as it operates in practice, reflects the interests of the dominant economic powers.

Developing states, on the other hand, have less capacity to protect the national interest in a context of globalization than the more powerful states. For the developing states, opening up also implies opening up to decisions taken in the capitals of developed countries, not because of some concern for international solidarity, but in defence of the local economy. In other words, economic globalization covers very different sets of relationships between states, each determined by the relative capacity of the 'partners'. Nayyar makes this point by qualifying economic interdependence as asymmetrical: 'There is a high degree of interdependence among countries in the industrialised world. There is considerable dependence of the developing countries on the industrialised countries. There is much less interdependence among countries in the developing world' (Nayyar 2002a: 7).

The dominant position of a number of developed states translates directly into political power in the context of decision-making practices in international economic organizations. The international financial institutions use a weighted voting system reflecting differences in quotas or shares. In both the IMF and the World Bank, the developed countries, and among them particularly the United States, dictate policy. Although in law the voting system in the World Trade Organization is different – based on consensus decision-making, and in the absence of consensus, on the base of one-member-one-vote – in practice industrialized countries dominate, given their grip on the organization of negotiation processes. Developing countries occasionally succeed, however, in blocking decision-making at the WTO. Historically, the culture of decision-making of international economic organizations is to pay tribute to the preferences of major economic powers and to aim at resolving disputes among those powers, rather than to strive for results that are as inclusive of all interests as possible. After all, in their relationships with developing countries, dominant economic powers still have the option not to use the multilateral level at all, and instead to go bilateral, a level at which relationships may be even more unequal.

Increasing the relevance of human rights

This book aims to contribute to the development of a theory of human rights that responds to some of the adverse impacts of economic globalization, particularly in the field of inequality. The proposition is that human rights are relevant as an instrument for fighting global injustice, but that it takes a conscious effort and commitment to develop human rights in such a way that they effectively address the social consequences of a globalizing economy. Some of the distrust of human rights within parts of the counter-movement to economic globalization comes from the perception that, after the Second World War, the West dominated the human rights discourse. Human rights came as part of a package that also included a preference for the free market economy and for a specific type of liberal democracy. This left a mark on how human rights concerns were prioritized. To some extent, that prioritization still prevails. As long as states remain important actors in international relations, it is inevitable that the practice of human rights is influenced by the national interests. States do not usually take a detached, cosmopolitan view of human rights issues, but instead decide on human rights issues in the context of a foreign policy that reflects domestic concerns.

In contrast, the purpose here is to take the adverse consequences of economic globalization as a starting point for

---

Box 2.2 UNDP: Required Shifts in Human Rights Thinking

- From the state-centred approaches to pluralist, multi-actor approaches – with accountability not only for the state but for media, corporations, schools, families, communities and individuals.
- From the national to international and global account-abilities – and from the international obligations of states to the responsibilities of global actors.
- From the focus on civil and political rights to a broader concern with all rights – giving as much attention to economic, social and cultural rights.
- From a punitive to a positive ethos in international pressure and assistance – from reliance on naming and shaming to positive support.
- From a focus on multiparty elections to the participation of all through inclusive models of democracy.
- From poverty eradication as a development goal to poverty eradication as social justice, fulfilling the rights and accountabilities of all actors.

Source: UNDP (2000: 13).

---

developing an adequate human rights response, regardless of the interests of one state, or of groups of states, such as the developing or the developed countries.

An important effort in this respect was the UNDP *Human Development Report 2000* focusing on human rights and human development. The report listed six shifts that were required to advance from the Cold War thinking on human rights, listed in Box 2.2.

Human rights do have the potential to fulfil Yash Ghai's promise of providing 'the nearest thing to a coherent challenge to economic globalization' (Ghai 1999: 130), but only if the current human rights regime develops in that specific direction.

The human rights regime includes all categories of human rights. Much of the literature on globalization and human rights tends to focus on economic, social and cultural (ESC) rights. This is understandable, as different aspects of social justice are matched by different ESC rights. There is also a need to improve the defence of ESC rights, given the tendency of the economically dominant actors to prioritize civil and political rights. Nevertheless, civil and political rights are important too in addressing the adverse consequences of economic globalization. Political rights suffer directly from a decline in the decision-making power of the state. Privatization not only affects social services, but also law enforcement and prisons. Freedom of expression and privacy rights are at the core of discussions about regulation of the internet, a major device facilitating the globalization of exchanges. The globalization and human rights debate thus does not concern only those convinced of the usefulness of ESC rights; it is equally relevant to those mainly preoccupied with civil and political rights.

The suggestions below are based, on the one hand, on the identification of elements within the current human rights regime that already offer protection against the adverse consequences of economic globalization, and, on the other hand, on proposals as to how the regime could be developed to offer more effective protection.

Adjust state obligations The human rights regime traditionally focuses on the state as the main duty holder. The assumption is that the state is the primary actor responsible for creating an environment that allows people to live in human dignity. Perhaps paradoxically, in the absence of its main violator, the human rights regime does not function.

The regime therefore certainly shares concerns about threats to the capacity of the state to manage the impact of economic globalization on its own territory, primarily because those threats also impact on the capacity of the state to ensure human dignity. The response has been to insist that even if states withdraw from the economy, their human rights obligations remain. For example, even if a state no longer directly provides an essential service such as the provision of healthcare, it remains responsible for the realization of the right to health. By necessity this implies a duty to oversee the activities of those who do provide the service, and to intervene when the performance of the service results in human rights violations.

The challenge to the human rights regime, then, is to adjust state obligations to a context where the role of the state as a social and economic actor is changing.

Extend human rights obligations to other actors The human rights regime has started to address relationships other than that between the state and the individuals that live on its territory. The recognition of the existence of human rights obligations of other actors contributes to the objective of ensuring that actors that in fact influence state policy and/or the quality of lives take responsibility *vis-à-vis* those affected.

The notion of extraterritorial human rights obligations – i.e. obligations of states that extend beyond their own borders to people in other states – opens up the possibility of addressing policy decisions taken by dominant states that adversely affect people in less powerful states. The construction of the human rights obligations of intergovernmental organizations, including of the international financial institutions, implies a challenge to the notion that these organizations are responsible only to their member-states. Human rights obligations of companies offer a partial response to the concern that regulation facilitating economic globalization is unbalanced in not addressing both the rights and obligations of investors. As non-governmental organizations become increasingly important actors in providing essential services to the poor, they too can no longer avoid responsibility for human rights, and it comes as no surprise that the debate about their accountability is picking up (Ebrahim 2003).

Recognize the primacy of human rights The notion of legal obligations is important in a human rights approach. Legal obligations restrict policy choices. Policy-makers must ensure that their choices are in conformity with human rights. Difficulties arise when human rights duty holders also accept other legal obligations, e.g. as states do, when they commit themselves to the framework of the World Trade Organization. Either in their wording or in effect, other obligations may contradict human rights obligations. Obviously this should not happen, but if it does, then it needs to be agreed that other legal obligations cannot limit the scope of human rights obligations. Only under these circumstances is the human rights regime useful as a corrective to the failures of governments and markets.

Establish credible accountability mechanisms One of the main assets of the human rights approach is the idea that human rights are real rights only if individuals are able to hold the duty holder accountable via a credible accountability mechanism. Downward accountability is essential to a human rights approach, and also of major importance for the protection of marginalized groups in the context of economic globalization. The human rights regime provides downward accountability mechanisms at domestic, regional and international levels, thus allowing interventions at the various levels that are relevant to economic globalization. Clearly, the international human rights regime constitutes one example of the use of international organizations for the achievement of non-market objectives.

Nevertheless, the credibility of existing accountability mechanisms varies. Marginalized groups face many barriers (including geographical and linguistic ones) in accessing such mechanisms. A credible downward accountability mechanism is based on clear rules against which behaviour can be tested, has the capacity to monitor behaviour, allows easy access to those claiming to be adversely affected, is capable of ensuring compliance and offers reparation when violations are established. The international human rights regime has a long way to go in establishing such mechanisms for human rights duty holders; for states, and even more for other actors.

Focus on those marginalized by state and market The human rights regime applies to all people, rich and poor. A slum dweller is no less worthy of protection than a tax consultant. Inclusiveness is essential to a human rights approach, and a welcome contrast to the exclusiveness inherent in the functioning of the market. The principle of non-discrimination is pivotal in ensuring equality in levels of protection, regardless of the economic status people enjoy in society. Women's rights require addressing gender inequalities that arise from economic globalization, not only through anti-discrimination measures, but also by pursuing policies that facilitate the access of women to the labour market.

In addition, the international human rights regime focuses in particular on grave abuses, on defining the core content of rights in order to ensure at least a minimum level of protection even to the worst off, and on groups requiring extra attention because of their vulnerability to violations. In brief, human rights provide a focus on individuals and groups that suffer the most abuse, and militate against a process that distributes the benefits and losses so unevenly as to deny individuals minimum levels of protection.

Think of rights in terms of social mobilization Groups that suffer abuse need to be able to defend themselves. They should not be reduced to victims in need of saving by others, or to mere beneficiaries of assistance. Groups can rely on freedom of expression and association to open up a political space where their claims can be heard, even in the face of more powerful forces that would wish to silence them. These freedoms are legal devices that, at least in principle, can be relied on before a judge. Even if this is not the case in practice, human rights are an important tool for social mobilization, because they contribute to the self-esteem of groups and individuals who may feel powerless due to their living conditions. The language of rights is empowering, even if the law fails. In the further development of human rights, due care should be taken not just of the potential of rights as a legal instrument, but also as an instrument of grassroots mobilization and political action.

Pluralize human rights In the era of economic globalization there is a need to reconcile the construction of rules at the international level with sufficient flexibility to avoid adverse consequences in a specific domestic context. The same need exists in the area of human rights. Human rights can contribute to more consideration of the consequences of international economic rules at the domestic level, if their own content reflects the realities of local human rights struggles. Otherwise human rights become one more instrument of homogenization. The challenge is to combine human rights rules that apply universally with varied interpretations that acknowledge the perceptions of local communities about the abuses they suffer.

Extend freedom of movement across borders The issue of free movement of persons offers another real challenge to the human rights regime. Free movement and the freedom to live where one wants are currently recognized rights, but only *inside* the state where a person resides lawfully. That person has the right to exit her state, but no right to enter any other state. States frequently argue that in order to realize the human rights of those who are in, others need to be kept out. International law, including human rights law, defers to the state's right to control the entry of foreign nationals. Even the UN Convention relating to the status of refugees does not offer a right of entry to those fulfilling the Convention's conditions. The Convention certainly does not envisage asylum for those applying for protection from a state that does not recognize that free mobility of labour is an inevitable component of economic globalization. Irregular migrants enjoy only minimal human rights protection, e.g. against disproportionate use of force. Some recognition of the need to ensure respect for the human rights of victims of trafficking has emerged. In limited circumstances the current human rights regime does facilitate entry, for instance in the context of family unification.

A more appropriate human rights response to the incentives economic globalization provides in favour of migration is to extend the freedom of movement across borders, shifting the burden of proof to states if they wish to impose limitations.

Human rights cannot address all concerns about economic globalization, nor can they address all aspects of these concerns. This is not to suggest that concerns about globalization, which human rights cannot address, are somehow less important; it simply means that they need to be tackled through other instruments.

One such issue is the unequal distribution of decision-making power among states in intergovernmental organizations. Human rights are not state rights. What is possible is to argue that notions that have been developed in the human rights context about political participation (transparency, accountability, respect for minority positions) should be extrapolated to cover voting procedures in intergovernmental organizations as well. Nevertheless, that argument is not a human rights argument as such, but an argument about best or minimum governance standards for intergovernmental organizations.

It can certainly be argued that human rights may contribute to addressing the adverse ecological consequences of economic globalization. Human rights enable individuals to challenge the impact of environmental degradation on their own lives. In the case law of the European Court of Human Rights, rights used for this purpose include the right to privacy, the right to family life, the right to information and the right to the peaceful enjoyment of one's possessions. In Latin America the individual human right to a healthy environment is receiving increasing recognition in both regional and domestic case law. In 2002, the Council of Europe published a 400-page book of international documents stressing the importance of human rights to the environment (Pallemaerts and Dejeant-Pons 2002). From the perspective of social mobilization, environmental human rights are useful in forging alliances between the environmental and the human rights movements.

Essentials

Nevertheless, many aspects of environmental degradation exceed the individual dimension, and although international environmental law has certainly been inspired by human rights law, particularly in its procedural aspects (rights to information, participation and remedies), it has also moved beyond human rights law in the protection that it offers. A pertinent example is the consolidation of the right of public participation in natural resource development, as exemplified in the 1998 UN/Economic Commission for Europe Aarhus Convention on access to information, public participation in decision-making and access to justice in environmental matters. The Aarhus Covention offers more detail on the right of public participation than international human rights law (Zillman et al. 2002). International economic organizations have been more willing to address the implications of international environmental law than of human rights law. Finally, the importance of the non-development, non-human rights angle of defending the value of the environment simply because of its inherent value should not be overlooked.

The market-friendly approach to human rights

The construction of human rights as an instrument addressing adverse consequences of economic globalization is not self-evident. It may not even be the dominant trend to perceive of human rights in this way. It is perfectly possible – through prioritization and selectivity – to construct a human rights theory that is fully compatible with or even supportive of economic globalization. International economic actors adopt this type of human rights discourse, and thus create distrust about the validity of human rights elsewhere.

The market-friendly approach to human rights prioritizes civil and political rights – the only real human rights, so the argument goes, because they are the only real legal rights. Aspects of civil and political rights are beneficial to a market economy. The rule of law, an independent judiciary, a government that is free from corruption, a free flow of information and the opportunity of choice for the consumer etc., are all necessary to ensure the proper functioning of the market. They are necessary everywhere, regardless of cultural context. Women's rights, too, are useful to the extent that they allow women to sell their services on the same terms as men, but not if they demand state resources or require market regulation, as in mandating parental leave or subsidized day-care (Rittich 2001: 103). Economic, social and cultural rights may exist, but they are long-term aspirations, the realization of which is dependent on economic growth, which in turn will result from the choice of the free market model. As long as the benefits of the process have not trickled down to the poor, there may be a need for the state to provide social safety-nets. There is no need to think about the human rights obligations of international economic organizations because this only complicates the operation of such organizations that have the potential to contribute to the realization of human rights as long as they are allowed to focus on their core business. If their policies somehow adversely touch on human rights, it is the domestic government's responsibility if it has ratified the relevant human rights treaties to take action. Companies that wish to accept social responsibility and engage in charity are to be congratulated, but no company should be obliged to do so. Monitoring of such policies should be left to the business community itself. Companies do not have human rights obligations. On the contrary: they are entitled to human rights protection. In any case, human rights should not become the cornerstone of international relations, i.e. the criterion against which every other rule is tested. Human rights are not at the top of the hierarchy of international rules. They are a legitimate concern to the extent that they do not impede the proper functioning of the market.

The difficulty with the market-friendly approach to human

rights is that it accepts the logic of the exclusiveness of the market. Markets have winners and losers, and it is the ability of the winners to reap the benefits that the market seeks to protect. Losers are not entitled to rewards, otherwise competition does not make sense. Social justice is at best a long-term objective that can be delayed indefinitely as long as the creation of growth remains the priority. Poverty needs to be contained, but will persist, if only because there will always be people that do not avail themselves of the opportunities the market offers. If the market is inclusive at all, it is in its encouragement to consume.

The market-friendly approach is detrimental to the human rights project. If any prioritization needs to take place, the only priority human rights recognize is gravity of abuse. Those who win the market game are not usually those who suffer the gravest violations. It is the people whom the market feels entitled to marginalize that are most vulnerable to violations. Human rights, if taken seriously, prioritize those excluded by the market and thus condemned to living in abhorrent conditions, to a life no marketeer would wish to contemplate. Most importantly, human rights need to challenge the mechanisms on which exclusion is based.

Inevitably, the conditions which expose people to human rights violations change. Today, one of those conditions is economic globalization. Human rights need to respond to the change; not so much in terms of their substance, but in terms of the relationships they cover. The human rights regime is not old. It is still growing up. Human rights must be a flexible, living instrument that can address new threats to human dignity, such as those flowing from economic globalization. Only then will they remain relevant. It is to that effort that this book seeks to contribute.

3 | Obstacles

Some characteristics of the human rights regime do not facilitate an appropriate human rights response to the adverse consequences of economic globalization.

Difficulties arise in two respects. Enforcing compliance of
human rights is not easy. Although human rights norms now
figure at international, regional and domestic levels, enforcement mechanisms are far from perfect. Having human rights
inscribed in law does not prevent violations, nor does the law
necessarily provide for effective accountability of perpetrators
to victims ('downward accountability'). Aggrieved individuals or
groups may feel deceived and frustrated when rights fail to deliver
on the promise their wording suggests.

Whether rights are respected may depend more on politics
than on any implementation mechanism. Politics reflect power
relations, and the politics of human rights falls victim to those
relationships. This applies domestically, but also at the international level. States that are dominant in military and economic
terms also dominate international human rights. The dominant
states defend their own foreign policy agenda in deciding whether
or not to push for compliance. Selectivity inevitably reflects on
the legitimacy of human rights as an issue of international
concern. A second difficulty flows from the limitations of treaty
law. The international human rights treaties of general scope
were adopted in the 1960s with a specific international context
– the Cold War – in mind. Treaties are difficult to touch. Any
suggestion that the international human rights covenants should
be amended immediately raises the spectre of losing all that
was gained.

After the 1960s, important new human rights treaties did emerge, e.g. on the rights of women and children, but they remained as state-orientated as the treaties of general application. The application of human rights treaties to actors other than the territorially responsible state requires reliance on intricate theories of interpretation. Not all human rights lawyers share enthusiasm for developing such theories. Some fear that the integrity of the content of the treaties may be lost, if the scope of the provisions is stretched, even if this is useful or necessary to address the adverse consequences of economic globalization. In addition, treaty lawyers tend to reduce human rights to their international legal content, refuting any application of the concept in circumstances not clearly recognized by international law.

Lack of compliance

The international level At the international level, the enforcement mechanisms of the human rights regime are weak. The UN Commission on Human Rights, the main UN political body dealing with human rights, adopts non-binding resolutions. The Commission's Special Rapporteurs and individual experts on countries and themes use strategies of naming and shaming. Their success depends on the vulnerability of the target state.

The committees established under the main human rights treaties to monitor compliance adopt a panoply of instruments: decisions, views, concluding observations ... all of which are recommendatory only, even if they enjoy considerable international standing. The instruments enable the committees to establish that violations have occurred and to suggest remedial action, but they do not bind states as Court judgments do. At best, a legitimate expectation exists that states will make every effort to comply with the committees' recommendations, as part of the duty to implement their treaty obligations in good faith. No compensation to victims is awarded. No sanctions are provided for, although the target state may suffer damage to its reputation. There is no international human rights court where individuals can hold states legally responsible. The International Criminal Court does have jurisdiction – under the conditions provided for in the statutes of the Court – over *persons* for the most serious crimes of international law including genocide, crimes against humanity and war crimes.

Weak monitoring mechanisms offer few incentives for compliance. Many a developing country is both a party to the main human rights conventions and a member of the World Trade Organization. As a consequence of WTO membership, states are under an obligation to amend their laws on the protection of intellectual property rights. At the same time, the relevant country is under an immediate obligation under the International Covenant on Economic, Social and Cultural Rights to ensure that there is no regress in the protection of the right to health. Let us assume that it is very difficult for the country to comply with both obligations at the same time. A pragmatic legal adviser to the government will no doubt compare the risks of non-compliance with both of the obligations. He or she is almost certain to advise that, if necessary, the human rights obligation should be ignored. At the end of the WTO dispute settlement system there are binding decisions, and economic sanctions in case of non-compliance. At the end of the human rights monitoring procedures there are recommendations, and more recommendations in case of non-compliance.

It would be unfair to suggest that no progress has been achieved over the last few decades. Individual complaint procedures have multiplied. The committees have clarified the content of state obligations under the different treaties, and become more focused in challenging state behaviour. Some of the Commission's rapporteurs and experts make or have made an impact. The trend towards increased individual responsibility for perpetrators of human rights violations is important, not least as part of a preventative strategy. The creation of the office of the UN High Commissioner for Human Rights (in the wake of the 1994 UN World Conference on Human Rights) contributed to the mainstreaming of human rights in the whole United Nations system.

The international level *is* important, particularly in the context of globalization. Global human rights require endorsement by an international forum, and this is what the UN human rights system provides. The formation of global alliances of social movements around human rights themes has been facilitated by the availability of UN human rights institutions and conferences. Such global alliances are in turn essential in moving towards downward accountability in a context where decisions are taken at many levels.

Nevertheless, the current international human rights regime still depends on constructive dialogue and cooperation. When a state fails to cooperate, and has sufficient capacity to resist diplomatic pressure, the human rights regime offers ritual condemnation at best. Those looking for a more muscular approach may look beyond the human rights regime to the UN Security Council. The UN Security Council can take into account the level of human rights violations in determining whether a threat to international peace and security exists that would warrant either economic or military sanctions. Needless to say, there is considerable controversy about the performance of the UN Security Council as a human rights defender.

Perhaps the major contribution of the international regime to better compliance is indirect. International bodies do influence state positions on human rights that may translate into domestic legislation. Individual complaint procedures are of particular importance in demonstrating to judges at regional and domestic levels that human rights are justiciable. From the grassroots perspective, this suggests a strategic use of the international complaints procedures. They offer little reparation to victims, except for the satisfaction of having a violation established. Ideally, cases taken should be exemplary, in that they go beyond the individual interest, and are of relevance beyond the boundaries of the respondent state. Cases should also stand a realistic chance of being won. Coordination among NGOs on the strategic use of the complaints procedures can certainly improve. The procedures are used optimally when the outcome is an international precedent that inspires judicial human rights activism at regional and domestic levels.

The regional level The regional human rights regime has a bit of everything. Strong human rights protection systems exist in the Americas and in Europe. Both systems have fully-fledged human rights courts that issue binding judgments on individual violations of the relevant regional human rights treaty. The inter-American system has the lowest threshold for petitions by individuals. The European Convention for the protection of human rights and fundamental freedoms fits within the framework of the Council of Europe, not of the European Union. The European Union treaty nevertheless commits the EU to respect for the rights in the Convention as general principles of European Community law.

The African Charter on Human and Peoples' Rights is distinctive from a normative perspective, but its main enforcement mechanism, the African Commission, has not performed effectively, nor did the Organization of African Unity (OAU) political bodies entrusted with the follow-up. The African human rights system suffers from a perennial lack of resources. The 1998 Protocol to the African Charter that envisages the establishment of an African Court of Human Rights has recently entered into force. The Charter is now linked to the new African Union. The

Assembly of the Heads of State of the AU plays a key role in the setting up of the court, including in the election of judges.

Asia and the Middle East do not have regional human rights protection systems. The United Nations cautiously promotes the establishment of regional arrangements in these parts of the world, but progress is tantalizingly slow. The UN has sponsored an infinite series of human rights seminars on regional coopera-tion in the Asia-Pacific region since 1982, but to little avail.

The contribution of sub-regional Asian organizations such as ASEAN and SAARC to human rights is modest as well. At the twelfth SAARC Summit, however, the organization adopted a new Social Charter (on 4 January 2004), which certainly deserves careful consideration.

A 1994 Arab Charter on Human Rights lies dormant. Not a single member-state of the League of Arab Nations ratified the treaty. Informal discussions have now commenced on modern-izing the text! In 1990, the Islamic Conference of Foreign Minis-ters adopted a solemn, but controversial and purely non-binding, Cairo Declaration on human rights in Islam.

The domestic level Avenues for enforcing human rights vary widely at the domestic level as well. International human rights treaties routinely require that rights are given effect at the domestic level. There are various ways in which states can comply with this obligation. Much depends on how the domestic legal system deals with international treaties in general. In some legal systems, ratification of a treaty suffices to make the treaty part of the law of the land.

In others, a treaty becomes part of domestic law only after it has been incorporated through an ordinary, domestic law. As long as incorporation has not occurred, the treaty remains largely out of reach for domestic enforcement mechanisms. A further problem is that a later domestic law may supersede the law incorporating the treaty. Judges can find a way around this by arguing that one should not assume that a domestic legislator had the intent to violate an international obligation unless the legislative history of the relevant bill shows so explicitly. In most instances, the law incorporating the treaty would thus prevail over the later law (Dugard 2000). Similarly, even if a treaty has not been incorporated, judges may wish to interpret domestic provisions in such a way as to avoid conflict.

As Scheinin points out, what counts in the last resort is the attitude of domestic judges, i.e. their willingness to give domestic effect to the international obligations of the state (Scheinin 1999: 421). The UN ESC Rights Committee recommends that 'judicial training should take full account of the justiciability of the Covenant'.[1] Whether judges in reality adopt an assertive attitude towards international human rights depends not only on their familiarity with international law, but also on their independence (i.e. whether they are free from improper pressure in decision-making) and if they have an impartial mind. In countries without a tradition of domestic human rights jurisprudence, an attitudinal change is required to encourage a judicial culture of service to the community, including to its marginalized sections. Oxner notes that attitudinal and thinking process change is the most difficult area of education. Results may not be easy to achieve, especially in a context where 'a starting judicial salary is equivalent to that of taxi driver', as in Pakistan (Oxner 2003: 332, 343).

International law is not the only source of domestic human rights obligations. Constitutions are no less important. Constitutions are the basic laws of the land, setting limitations on the exercise of sovereignty by the ruler. They increasingly include human rights catalogues, often inspired by international norms. Domestic legal systems often provide mechanisms for testing the validity of actions and/or legislation against the constitution.

Box 3.1 On the Judgment of the South African Constitutional Court in the Case of the Government of the Republic of South Africa and Others v. Irene Grootboom and Others, *case no. CCT 11/00 (4 October 2000)*

The *Grootboom* case was brought by 900 people who had put up shacks and shelters on vacant land that was privately owned. After a few months, the private owner obtained an eviction order, and the people were forcibly removed. They then camped on a sports field in the area, under temporary structures consisting of plastic sheets. Article 26 of the South African constitution provides for the right to have access to adequate housing. The provision includes a duty on the state 'to take reasonable legislative and other measures, within its available resources, to achieve the progressive realization of this right'. According to the Constitutional Court, the constitution did not guarantee a state obligation to provide basic shelter immediately upon demand, but it did require a housing programme with measures that were reasonable both in their conception and implementation. A measure would pass the reasonableness test if it was comprehensive and well coordinated, was capable of facilitating the right in question progressively, was balanced, did not exclude a significant segment of society, and responded to the urgent needs of people who had no access to land, no roof over their heads, and who were living in intolerable conditions or crisis situations. In the present case, it was unreasonable that the nationwide housing programme failed to recognize that the state must provide for relief for those in desperate need. The Court ordered the government to include such relief measures in its housing programme.

Even constitutions may be ignored, however. Hyden and Venter find that in Africa constitutions have seldom played their attributed role, although they discern a positive trend during the last decade, citing the examples of South Africa, Uganda, Ethiopia and Eritrea (Hyden and Venter 2001).

Not all constitutions are transformative in that they challenge long-standing practices in the society. Some distinguish between categories of rights, perceiving civil and political rights as fundamental, and economic and social rights as mere directive principles of state policy, leaving the responsibility for the fulfilment of these rights to legislative and administrative bodies only, and not to the judiciary (Agbakwa 2002: 186). Indian constitutional law, as interpreted by the Indian Supreme Court, adopts a middle position. Although the constitution includes only ESC rights as directive principles, the Court has interpreted civil and political rights (which are justiciable) in the light of these principles, and has thus equated the right to life with a right to live with human dignity, including a minimum protection of health and social security rights for workers. The South African Constitutional Court currently performs a key role in demonstrating the judicial enforceability of economic, social and cultural rights.

Constitutional human rights provisions may well be insufficient if they remain limited to declaring broad principles. Often, legislation will be needed to determine what exactly is expected in terms of procedures and accountability of governmental implementing agencies. Non-judicial bodies also have an important role in this respect. The ombudsman is an independent official who is deemed to act informally and quickly in response to individual complaints about the performance of the civil service. National human rights commissions may have wide powers including the monitoring of government policies, advising on legislative reform, providing human rights education, or even the right of initiative to undertake investigations of their

39

own. The South African human rights commission appeared as a friend of the court in the *Grootboom* case. The degree of independence of national Human Rights Commissions determines their effectiveness as a domestic enforceability mechanism (Von Tigerstrom 2001).

An interesting new development from Brazil is the appoint-

---

*Box 3.2 1987 Philippine Constitution: Article XIII on
the Establishment of the Commission on Human Rights
(in part)*

Section 17

1 There is hereby created an independent office called the Commission on Human Rights.

2 The Commission shall be composed of a Chairman and four Members who must be natural-born citizens of the Philippines and a majority of whom shall be members of the Bar. The term of office and other qualifications and disabilities of the Members of the Commission shall be provided by law [...]

Section 18

The Commission on Human Rights shall have the following powers and functions:

1 Investigate, on its own or on complaint by any party, all forms of human rights violations involving civil and political rights.

2 Adopt its operational guidelines and rules of procedure, and cite for contempt for violations thereof in accordance with the Rules of Court.

3 Provide appropriate legal measures for the protection of human rights of all persons within the Philippines, as well

---

ment of domestic special rapporteurs, modelled on the Commission's system. A civil society network called the 'Brazilian Platform for Economic, Social and Cultural Human Rights' (Plataforma Brasileira de Direitos Humanos Econômicos, Sociais e Culturais) originated the system in October 2002. Six rapporteurs were appointed by various non-governmental, state and UN

---

as Filipinos residing abroad, and provide for preventive measures and legal aid services to the under-privileged whose human rights have been violated or need protection.

4 Exercise visitorial powers over jails, prisons, or detention facilities.

5 Establish a continuing programme of research, education and information to enhance respect for the primacy of human rights.

6 Recommend to Congress effective measures to promote human rights and to provide for compensation to victims of violations of human rights, or their families.

7 Monitor the Philippine Government's compliance with international treaty obligations on human rights.

8 Grant immunity from prosecution to any person whose testimony or whose possession of documents or other evidence is necessary or convenient to determine the truth in any investigation conducted by it or under its authority.
[...]

Section 19
The Congress may provide for other cases of violations of human rights that should fall within the authority of the Commission, taking into account its recommendations.

Obstacles

organizations. According to the network, the rapporteurs work independently and in close cooperation with broad sectors of society to perform exemplary monitoring of the human rights situation in Brazil. A large number of social groups reportedly participate in the hearings and contribute to the compilation of the reports.[2]

Selective use and interpretation

Gilpin argues that compliance problems are inevitable for international regimes that 'have significant distributive consequences for states and powerful domestic groups, or [...] impinge significantly on the autonomy and security of states' (Gilpin 2001: 89). The human rights regime certainly fits this category. Compliance problems occur because there is no authoritative international government, and because states give priority to their domestic agenda. Since the regime itself lacks the power to enforce compliance, Gilpin's view is that the only alternative is strong international leadership of a hegemonic state (or group of states) that facilitates cooperation and prevents defection from the rules of the regime (ibid., p. 97). The history of the international politics of human rights shows that the developed states have been eager to heed Gilpin's call, but arguably with detrimental effects on the validity of human rights as a legitimate international concern everywhere else. The damage was done not only because other states resent the dominant attitude of the West, but also because the hegemonic powers' concern for human rights is influenced by other parts of their foreign policy agenda.

The Universal Declaration of Human Rights contains both civil and political rights, and economic, social and cultural rights. In 1966 a split between the two groups of rights occurred. Two separate treaties were created: the International Covenant on Civil and Political Rights, with an optional protocol providing for an individual complaints procedure, and the International Covenant on Economic, Social and Cultural Rights that had no meaningful monitoring procedure. During the Cold War each bloc favoured its own set of rights, and did battle. The NGO human rights movement was able to develop in the West only, and focused almost exclusively on civil and political rights. Legal arguments were found to support the split. Civil and political rights were justiciable because they entailed immediate, negative obligations with little resource implications. Economic, social and cultural rights were policy prescriptions only, because they represented long-term aspirations and were heavily dependent on the availability of resources.

The decision to separate the two sets of rights held the international human rights effort in a deadlock for decades. No progress was achieved for the duration of the Cold War. Those sharing the ideology of one bloc but living in the other were deprived of human rights protection. In the South, human rights were associated with the security and economic agendas of the North. The split isolated human rights from development efforts, as resource levels were not deemed to be important to the one category of rights that really mattered.

It took a while to rebut the legal arguments as well. Today there is agreement that both sets of rights require abstention and intervention. Whether states need to commit resources for the realization of human rights does not depend on whether the right is civil, cultural, economic, political or social; it depends on the nature of the obligation. Not demolishing a house does not cost money, while providing training to a judge does. At the United Nations, the gap between the two sets of rights has been closed over the last decade, at least rhetorically. According to the 1993 World Conference on Human Rights, the international community must treat human rights globally in a fair and equal manner, on the same footing and with the same emphasis. It is an

43

important statement. Both sets of rights are mutually dependent in reality. At the global level, there is no consensus on human rights except if equal attention is given to both sets. Attempts at establishing a hierarchy are deeply divisive.

The end of the Cold War did not close the book on concerns about the use of human rights as an instrument of Western dominance. Makau Mutua argues that the campaign to universalize human rights presents a historical continuum in an unbroken chain of Western conceptual and cultural dominance over the last century. The globalization of human rights fits a historical pattern in which all high morality comes from the West as a civilizing agent against lower forms of civilization: 'It forms a long queue of the colonial administrator, the Bible-wielding Christian missionary, the merchant of free enterprise, the exporter of political democracy, and now the human rights zealot' (Mutua 2002: 20). The human rights movement, he argues, is marked by a damning savages–victims–saviour metaphor, where the savage is the non-white state, the victim a helpless non-white innocent and the saviours are the United Nations, Western governments, international non-governmental organizations and Western charities.

Upendra Baxi too speaks of the all too common perception that human rights are 'gifts of the West to the rest' (Baxi 2002: vi). Both authors adopt what Mutua calls an 'outsider–insider perspective' on the human rights movement. They subscribe to the validity of the human rights discourse, but reject the imposition of a purely Western interpretation of human rights and insist on equality in the taking into account of multiple Western and non-Western experiences in the formulation of the normative content of genuinely universal human rights. In Mutua's words:

> The only hope for those who care about the adherence by all communities to human rights is the painstaking study of each culture to identify norms and ideals that are in consonance with

universal standards. Only by *locating* the basis for the cultural legitimacy of certain human rights and mobilizing social forces on that score can respect for universal standards be forged. (Mutua 2002: 81)

Inevitably, states that dominate other areas of international relations also dominate the politics of human rights. The debate on whether human rights are individual rights only offers an illustration. The mainstream Western view is that human rights by definition are individual rights. Consequently, little has been achieved in terms of recognizing or operating group rights at the international level. If non-Western societies had been dominant in formulating the international discourse on human rights, individuals would have been approached much more as social beings. Arguably, international human rights would not just have regulated the relationship between the state and the individual, but would also have dealt with how both the state and the individual relate to the intermediate level of the groups (families, communities, age groups) that determine the social position of the individual.

Similarly, states that are economically dominant push for a market-friendly approach to human rights. Western states resist recognizing group rights as rights with the argument that human rights belong to individuals as humans, and thus cannot be collective, but see little difficulty in recognizing corporate rights as human rights. In 2002, the European Court of Human Rights unanimously held that 'the time had come' to acknowledge that a number of road construction companies had a 'home' as protected under the right to privacy. The case concerned a fraud investigation that involved wide powers for the investigating offices to enter the companies' premises and seize documents.[3] Whatever one's view of the fairness of the investigation procedure, the attribution of human rights to corporations raises

Obstacles

serious concerns about the integrity of the human rights concept. If corporations have human rights too, there is no guarantee that in case of conflict between the human right of the corporate entity and the human right of the human being, the latter right will prevail. When human rights are attributed to companies, they become one more tool for expanding the private sphere in which companies can operate without state intervention.

In a similar vein, the 'fundamental freedoms' in the new draft constitution of the European Union are not the human rights that one might have expected under that heading, but the 'free movement of persons, goods, services and capital, and freedom of establishment'. The draft constitution does not appear to distinguish the legal value of these fundamental freedoms from the fundamental rights that follow a little later in the text.[4] In a paper on the International Covenant on Economic, Social and Cultural Rights, the General Counsel of the International Monetary Fund, another advocate of the market-friendly approach to human rights, charges that the Covenant appears 'somewhat removed from the realities of today's internally and externally open economy'. Important rights such as the right to own property, the right to engage in economic activity and to trade are missing.[5]

Under the complaints procedure of the International Covenant on Civil and Political Rights, only individuals can submit a communication; companies have no standing.[6] Perhaps the time has not yet come at the international level, but it will, if the advocates of the market-friendly approach to human rights have their way.

The challenge is to ensure that human rights do not evolve into a tool for protecting the interests of the dominant political and economic powers but, on the contrary, strengthen their inclusiveness by increasingly acknowledging the experiences of those marginalized by dominant forces. Baxi speaks of people in struggle and communities of resistance as the originary authors of human rights (Baxi 2002: vi). The mission of contemporary human rights is to give voice to human suffering, to make it visible and to ameliorate it. He envisages a process in which 'resistance to power has a creationist role in the making of "contemporary" human rights, which then at a second order level, get translated into standards and norms adopted by a community of states. In the making of human rights it is the local that translates into global languages the reality of their aspiration for a just world' (ibid., p. 101).

Tied by treaty

Article 2, par. 1 of the International Covenant on Economic, Social and Cultural Rights defines the legal nature of state obligations under the treaty. With a few notable exceptions, the clause is of general application to the rights enumerated in the treaty: 'Each state Party to the present Covenant undertakes to take steps, individually and through international assistance and co-operation, especially economic and technical, to the maximum of its available resources, with a view to achieving progressively the full realization of the rights recognized in the present Covenant by all appropriate means, including particularly the adoption of legislative measures.' Anyone reading the provision for the first time must wonder what it means. What specific obligations does the clause impose on ratifying states? The original state response was that this standard of progressive realization amounted to a commitment to make an effort, but did not require the attainment of a specific result. Leading commentators describe the clause as 'a loophole large enough in practical terms to nullify the Covenant's guarantees' (Chapman and Russell 2002: 5). Certainly Article 2, par. 1 is not an example of inspired drafting. The wording is so complex that it enables various interpretations – some kind to ESC rights, others not. In any case, the drafters

47

rendered a service to states wishing to deny all justiciability to these rights.

The meaning of the provision has now been clarified in a number of general comments of the UN Committee on ESC Rights, the body that monitors state compliance with the treaty. The committee has said that all the rights in the Covenant entail minimum core obligations to ensure the satisfaction of, at the very least, minimum essential levels of each of the rights: 'a state party in which any significant number of individuals is deprived of essential foodstuffs, of essential primary health care, of basic shelter and housing, or of the most basic forms of education, is *prima facie* failing to discharge its obligations under the Covenant'.[7]

The committee takes the position that there is no Covenant right which could not, in the great majority of legal systems, 'possess at least some significant justiciable dimensions'.[8] The committee has gone to great lengths to develop a typology of state obligations attaching to the various rights: the state should not take away resources that are essential for people to provide for their own rights (e.g. by taking away land on which people grow their own food); the state should provide protection against abuse by third parties (e.g. by requiring from companies that they provide safe working conditions); and in life-threatening situations should fulfil the right (e.g. by providing food during a famine; cf. Sepulveda 2003: 174). The committee's inspired efforts have removed the ambiguity of the original clause.

Nevertheless, the text of the clause remains as it was, physically separated from the committee's vital clarifications. From a strictly legal point of view, the committee's general comments are not binding, although governments and judges are well advised to acknowledge their authority. The legal state of affairs has not escaped the attention of the IMF General Council. When discussing the committee's view on duties of international cooperation in the Covenant, he subtly alerts states that they have a choice in deciding whether or not they share the committee's interpretation. Perhaps more importantly, the awkward wording of the Covenant affects the practical usefulness of the document. It is not sufficient to convince a sceptical government official responsible for housing policy that she has immediate obligations even if the text of the treaty does not explicitly state them. Of course, reference can be made to the general comments of the Committee on ESC Rights ('this is what the text really means'), but many a government official will be unfamiliar with the Geneva Committee, and may well doubt its relevance. The ambiguity of the treaty provision shifts the burden away from the government official who is under pressure to justify the quality of the domestic housing policy to the person invoking human rights, who is challenged to prove the applicability of the international text.[9]

Two other aspects of human rights treaties may be seen as limiting their usefulness in addressing economic globalization. One is the state orientation of the treaties. The second is their territorial scope.

State orientated States ratify human rights treaties. Ratification implies consent to be bound. Other actors, such as international organizations and companies, are barred from ratifying the treaties (even if they wanted to), and thus can be bound only indirectly. Human rights primarily regulate the vertical relationship between the state and the individual. The horizontal application of human rights in the relationships between individuals, including the possibility of one individual enforcing his or her rights against another, is unusual.

Some human rights treaties explicitly provide for a state obligation to legislate or even to penalize the behaviour of others within its jurisdiction. The Convention on the Elimination of All Forms of Discrimination Against Women thus requires that

Box 3.3 *Supreme Court of India,* Consumer Education and Research Centre v. Union of India, *Judgment of 27 January 1995, pars 26, 33 (in part)*

26. [...] Therefore, it must be held that the right to health and medical care is a fundamental right under Article 21 read with Articles 39(c), 41 and 43 of the Constitution and make the life of the workman meaningful and purposeful with dignity of person. Right to life includes protection of the health and strength of the worker, is a minimum requirement to enable a person to live with human dignity. The State, be it Union or State Government or an industry, public or private, is enjoined to take all such action which will promote health, strength and vigour of the workman during the period of employment and leisure and health even after retirement as basic essentials to live the life with health and happiness.

33. [...] All the industries are directed: (1) To maintain and keep maintaining the health record of every worker up to a minimum period of 40 years from the beginning of the employment or 15 years after retirement or cessation of the employment whichever is later; (2) The Membrane Filter test, to detect asbestos fibre should be adopted by all the factories or establishments at par with the Metalliferrous Mines Regulations, 1961; and Vienna Convention and Rules issued thereunder; (3) All the factories whether covered by the Employees' State Insurance Act or Workmen's Compensation Act or otherwise are directed to compulsorily insure health coverage to every worker.

states take appropriate steps to eliminate discrimination against women *by any person, organization or enterprise*. The state also needs to take measures to modify the social and cultural patterns of conduct of men and women with a view to achieving the elimination of prejudices. The treaty further adds that steps and measures include the adoption of legislation, including sanctions, where appropriate. The Convention on the Elimination of Racial Discrimination includes a state obligation to declare punishable by law the dissemination of ideas based on racial superiority or hatred.[10]

The states are obliged to complement the treaties with domestic legislation regulating the behaviour of all those within the state's jurisdiction. This division of labour between international law and domestic law is a traditional one. International law does not ordinarily intervene in the relationship between two private actors, such as a company and a local community. Nothing prevents states from enacting human rights obligations for private actors within the domestic legal system, but they are only exceptionally (as in the examples mentioned) under an international obligation to do so. In a climate of competition for investment, incentives may not be high for enacting corporate human rights obligations. Nevertheless, the Indian Supreme Court has been willing to provide constitutional human rights protection against acts by private actors or industry.

In response to a number of individual complaints, international and regional courts or monitoring bodies emphasized that states do have an obligation to offer protection to persons under their jurisdiction whose rights are threatened by others. The duty to protect is included in all categories of rights, although most of the cases involved alleged violations of civil and political rights. In the *Vélasquez Rodrigues* case (see Box 3.4), the Inter-American Court of Human Rights found that Honduras had not done enough to prevent or investigate a disappearance.

Box 3.4   Inter-American Court of Human Rights, Vélasquez-Rodrigues v. Honduras *(no. 7920), Judgment of 29 July 1988, pars 172–7 (in part)*

172. [...] An illegal act which violates human rights and which is initially not directly imputable to a State (for example, because it is the act of a private person or because the person responsible has not been identified) can lead to international responsibility of the State, not because of the act itself, but because of the lack of due diligence to prevent the violation or to respond to it as required by the Convention.

173. [...] What is decisive is whether a violation of the rights recognized by the Convention has occurred with the support or the acquiescence of the government, or whether the State has allowed the act to take place without taking measures to prevent it or to punish those responsible. Thus, the Court's task is to determine whether the violation is the result of a State's failure to fulfill its duty to respect and guarantee those rights, as required by Article 1 (1) of the Convention.

174. The State has a legal duty to take reasonable steps to prevent human rights violations and to use the means at its disposal to carry out a serious investigation of violations committed within its jurisdiction, to identify those responsible, to impose the appropriate punishment and to ensure the victim adequate compensation.

175. This duty to prevent includes all those means of a legal, political, administrative and cultural nature that promote the protection of human rights and ensure that any violations are considered and treated as illegal acts, which, as such,

may lead to the punishment of those responsible and the obligation to indemnify the victims for damages [...]

177. In certain circumstances, it may be difficult to investigate acts that violate an individual's rights. The duty to investigate, like the duty to prevent, is not breached merely because the investigation does not produce a satisfactory result. Nevertheless, it must be undertaken in a serious manner and not as a mere formality preordained to be ineffective. An investigation must have an objective and be assumed by the State as its own legal duty, not as a step taken by private interests that depends upon the initiative of the victim or his family or upon their offer of proof, without an effective search for the truth by the government. This is true regardless of what agent is eventually found responsible for the violation. Where the acts of private parties that violate the Convention are not seriously investigated, those parties are aided in a sense by the government, thereby making the State responsible on the international plane.

Nothing prevents the application of the Inter-American Court's due diligence standard to a case involving violations of the rights of members of a community as a consequence of a private company's extraction activities. A finding that a state violated the due diligence obligation by not taking measures to prevent the violations and indemnify victims afterwards, inevitably implies that the private actor's behaviour was abusive of human rights. Such a finding, however, stops short of distributing the responsibility between the state and the private actor, or of holding the private actor independently responsible. Scott proposes that shared responsibility for human rights violations between public and

Obstacles

private actors should become possible, suggesting that a careful analysis of fields of responsibility and power relations between both actors should allow deciding an appropriate allocation of the responsibility and remedies (Scott 2001: 31). Similarly, Clapham and Jerbi develop a theory of corporate complicity, distinguishing between direct, beneficial and silent complicity (Clapham and Jerbi 2001). Such theories bring the promise of the preamble of the Universal Declaration of Human Rights a step closer, namely that human rights are a common standard of achievement not just for states and individuals, but also for 'every organ of society'.

Individual criminal responsibility for human rights violations is relevant to corporate behaviour. The Statute of the International Criminal Court does not provide for corporate responsibility as such, but managers of a corporation can be held individually accountable for crimes as defined in the statute. This is not new law. After the Second World War, the military tribunal at Nuremberg convicted directors of German companies for their involvement in war crimes.

Bound by borders A major concern arising from globalization is that state policies, and in particular those of non-dominant states, are increasingly affected by decisions made elsewhere. Decisions by intergovernmental organizations or by other states may adversely affect the human rights of people who are not under their territorial control, and to whom they are not accountable.

In human rights treaty law, each state is obliged to ensure the human rights of individuals only within its own territory and subject to its own jurisdiction. The international human rights system legitimizes the expression of concern or even the taking of action by one state over violations occurring elsewhere, but the system is not based on solidarity. States have *obligations* towards the people within their borders only.

Consequently, it is not easy to argue that rich states are somehow responsible for human rights violations occurring in poor states, either directly or through the policies they sponsor within the international economic organizations. An extraterritorial or transnational (Skogly and Gibney 2002) reach of human rights obligations requires special circumstances or reliance on the few human rights treaty provisions that offer an inroad.

In a limited number of international and regional cases, states were held responsible for human rights violations occurring outside their own territory. Not all human rights treaties use the same language in defining the territorial scope of state obligations, and consequently the case law of each institution is somewhat different. The European Court of Human Rights accepts that a state is responsible for what happens in another territory, if that state 'through the effective control of the relevant territory and its inhabitants abroad as a consequence of military occupation or through the consent, invitation or acquiescence of the Government of that territory, exercises all or some of the public powers normally to be exercised by that Government'.[11] The Court does not accept, however, that 'anyone adversely affected by an act imputable to a Contracting State, wherever in the world that act may have been committed or its consequences felt, is thereby brought within the jurisdiction of that State'. In the case under review, the consequence was that Belgium and nine other NATO states involved in military operations against Serbia could not be held responsible for killings of civilians that occurred as a consequence of the bombing of the Serb Radio and Television building in Belgrade. The Court pointed out that the European Convention was a mere regional instrument, not designed to be applied throughout the world, even in respect of the conduct of states that had ratified it.

The Inter-American Commission of Human Rights was willing to look into the detention and treatment by US forces of prisoners

Box 3.5 FIAN, Bread for the World, Church Development Service (2001), Parallel Report on Germany: the Right to Adequate Food, pars 51–2

51. The Committee should ask in its concluding observations the government of Germany to add in future to its state reports a specific chapter on international obligations. In this chapter Germany should submit:

- An assessment of the outcome of its own policies affecting vulnerable people in other countries, which includes finance, aid, trade, and agricultural policies. At the same time the respective parallel EU policies must be checked, especially the outcome of trade and agricultural policies on vulnerable people in other countries.
- An assessment of the outcome of own aid-policies, the influence of decisions of its export credit agency and its debt policy.
- A reflection about its role in international organizations and about possible conflicts between Germany's obligations under Human Rights law and under other international regimes.
- A report, how Germany will analyse in future the outcome of policies and programmes of the WTO, IMF, World Bank and other intergovernmental institutions on vulnerable people in other countries.

The overall objective of this endeavour would be that it becomes a routine for States Parties to report on the compliance with their international obligations.

52. The Committee should ask the government of Germany, in which way Germany currently carries out these assess-

ments, in particular with respect to its agricultural and trade policies:

- its fishery policy
- its export credit insurance
- its aid policy
- its role in the WTO and the International Financial Institutions

during the first days of the military campaign in Grenada because the prisoners were subject to the authority and control of the United States.[12] The Inter-American Commission applied the same reasoning when it ordered the United States urgently to enable a competent tribunal to determine the legal status of the detainees at Guantanamo Bay,[13] only to find its order ignored. The UN Human Rights Committee held Uruguay responsible for a kidnapping perpetrated by its security and intelligence forces in Argentina, arguing that it 'would be unconscionable [...] to permit a State party to perpetrate violations of the Covenant on the territory of another State, which violations it could not perpetrate on its own'.[14]

In these cases extraterritorial human rights responsibility is envisaged only when individuals are under the effective control of (agents of) another state. There is no effective control when a developed country votes for a World Bank decision that subsequently adversely affects human rights elsewhere. If any responsibility arises, it is of the cause-and-effect type that the European Court did not wish to entertain. But even if a cause-and-effect theory for establishing responsibility across borders were to be accepted, one would still need to demonstrate the causal link between the vote in the Bank's decision-making bodies and

57

the subsequent human rights violations in the borrower country. No doubt the defence would argue that no such link can be established given the sovereignty of the state on whose territory the contested project takes place. The borrower country remains responsible for managing the project, including a responsibility to prevent human rights violations if the project entails human rights risks.

For the moment at least, judicial institutions are unlikely to extend extraterritorial responsibility to actors taking decisions that affect human rights elsewhere. The UN Committee on Economic, Social and Cultural Rights, however, has more room for manoeuvre when it investigates state reports on their compliance with the Covenant. The International Covenant on Economic, Social and Cultural Rights repeatedly refers to the need to achieve ESC rights 'through international assistance and cooperation', as it does in Article 2 quoted above. According to the committee: 'Where a state party is clearly lacking in the financial resources and/or expertise required [...] the international community has a clear obligation to assist.'[15] The reverse side of the coin is a duty for states to abstain from any policy that impinges on the protection of at least the core content of the economic, social and cultural rights of the affected peoples of another state.[16] Consequently, the committee has started gently questioning developed states on whether their participation in intergovernmental organizations is in conformity with their duties of international cooperation under the Covenant, and in its concluding observations has encouraged them to ensure that it is. Non-governmental organizations have also initiated reporting on how donor countries influence human rights elsewhere in their alternative reports to the committee.

Customary law One avenue for escaping the limitations of treaty law is reliance on another source of international law:

customary law. Humanitarian lawyers are used to this escape route. The humanitarian law treaties are replete with threshold requirements severely limiting their applicability to modern conflicts. The response, which international tribunals increasingly endorse, is that the content of treaty obligations has now become customary law, and that therefore states and other actors are also bound by the substance of the rules in circumstances in which the treaties do not apply as such. Reliance on customary law, or on the related category of general principles of international law, allows for the extension of basic humanitarian protection in circumstances not envisaged at the time when the treaties were drafted.

A similar approach also exists in international human rights law, although it is arguably less developed than in humanitarian law. There is a debate about which human rights obligations have achieved the status of customary law or of general principles. The International Court of Justice has not ruled on whether the Universal Declaration of Human Rights has reached this status. The ICJ has made statements on specific human rights that were relevant to the case before the Court, such as the protection from slavery, the prohibition of racial discrimination, the wrongful deprivation of freedom and the right to self-determination (which, interestingly, in the context of globalization includes a prohibition to deprive a people of its own means of subsistence), as belonging to the 'general rules of international law'. Rules in this category definitely apply to intergovernmental organizations. Consequently, the international financial institutions are subject to the reach of human rights law in so far as human rights law has attained the status of general rules. Skogly makes an appealing argument in favour of an approach suggesting that *aspects of* most civil, cultural, economic, political and social rights have attained the status of general rules (Skogly 2001: 120–3).

Limited by law

A final difficulty is that, as in the domination of development studies by economists, the legal discipline tends to dominate human rights analysis. Legal mechanisms are perceived of as being by far the most important, if not the only, instruments for providing human rights protection.

It is problematic to rely solely upon legal measures and litigation for the protection of human rights. Most litigation in developing countries involves either business or the propertied classes, and it follows that the supply of legal services tends to reflect the preferences and needs of their most common users. Poor people are rarely able to use formal legal systems to pursue their claims: 'The actual costs of engaging a lawyer, the opportunity cost of time spent in court, and the general level of skill and education required to litigate effectively, all serve as deterrents' (DFID 2000: 11). In countries with high illiteracy rates, the requirement of a written complaint denies access to those most vulnerable to human rights violations. Often, changes in domestic procedural law are required if litigation is to be an effective instrument for the poor. The availability of autonomous legal aid foundations targeting the poor is essential (Khor and Li Lin 2001: 222). International and regional enforcement mechanisms are even more difficult to access than domestic ones, in part because complaints tend to be admissible only after domestic remedies have been exhausted.

Falk Moore identifies 'a striking difference' between two currents of human rights talk: one reflecting the theoretical debates surrounding the worldwide human rights movement on defining universally applicable standards ('what should be'); the other interested in the specific description of what is happening on the ground in terms of contestations over rights ('what is'). She points out that human rights discussions in the abstract seem aimless without a concomitant discussion of the practical conditions – including reflections on prevailing political and economic inequities – under which action can be taken (Falk Moore 1999). Lessons need to be learned from how human rights function in reality at the local level. An understanding of the local circumstances which determine whether protection will be real is essential for improving the relevance of the international standards and mechanisms. Such an understanding cannot be gained by reference to the legal discipline only.

One analysis points out, for instance, that the impact of the *Grootboom* case (referred to above) on housing policy in South Africa has not been dramatic (Pillay 2002). The members of the community who brought the case received a one-off payment allowing them to buy basic materials for housing, but the provision of municipal services to the area remains unresolved. More than a year after the judgment was handed down, no visible change in housing policy as it affects people in desperate situations had reportedly occurred. Doubts remained about political commitment at all relevant levels of government to a systemic change in policy as required by the judgment. On the other hand, additional judgments in the wake of *Grootboom* are of practical assistance in improving living conditions, if only of those bringing the case (Mahomed 2003). Clearly, even in as beneficial a legal context as the South African one, a strategy based on litigation alone is insufficient to produce fundamental change.

The more fundamental issue is as follows. Law is an institutionalized power resource that lends itself to many uses. In most legal systems around the world, lawyers simply translate decisions taken by others into a legal framework. International human rights law is a product of the community of states, and human rights lawyers will often accept the limitation of working within that framework. Lawyers tend to reduce the debate about human rights to a debate on the scope of the protection provided for under the current legal framework. This is important, as it does make a difference whether or not a given claim has achieved recognition under international or domestic human rights law. It is equally important to strive towards achieving the widest possible protection under the current law. The UN Committee on Economic, Social and Cultural Rights' efforts to strengthen protection under the Covenant are a good example.

A problem arises, however, if human rights end where current human rights *law* ends. As a product of the community of states, international human rights law is imperfect. International law is unable to change deep-rooted attitudes, as feminists found when studying the impact of law on patriarchy (Macdonald 2003: 12). Baxi points out that over the years the 'lawyer's law' of human rights has been perfectly compatible with structural violations. Human rights law had no difficulty in excluding hosts of humans as beneficiaries from protection: slaves, heathens, barbarians, colonized peoples, women and so on. Today, human rights law accepts as legitimate 'the affluence of a few with the extreme impoverishment of many, locally and globally' (Baxi 2002: 8) or the denial of freedom of movement across borders. To the extent that international human rights law simply reflects dominant interests, it contributes to making specific categories of human suffering invisible. Important progress still needs to be made in achieving the full inclusiveness of human rights protection, and the law should not function as an instrument of restricting human rights to what has proved politically acceptable so far.

International law faces methodological difficulties in creating space for an approach inspired by human suffering. There is no technique for taking into account the consequences of legal rules for those who do not have a powerful voice in the legal system. 'Texts of resistance' are not a source of international law (Rajagopal 2003: 233). The history of human rights is told through major legal decisions, rather than by telling the story of societal struggles that initiate change. As Rajagopal suggests:

'Engaging with the theory and practice of social movements is necessary to convert human-rights discourse from its narrow, state-centered, elitist basis to a grassroots-oriented praxis of the subalterns' (ibid., p. 271).

Rajagopal´s view is fully in line with Baxi's perception of people and communities in struggle as the originary authors of human rights. Both writers also stress the need to 'convert' or 'translate' the experiences of these communities into international law. Other actors need to make a contribution to this process of translation as well. Technically, international law requires their intervention, since only states and intergovernmental organizations have the authority to set rules.

There may be other reasons why translation is appropriate. People who have suffered human rights violations are not necessarily able to empathize with other groups that have suffered similar injustice. In a doctoral thesis on victim organizations in Rwanda, Heidy Rombouts (2004: 329) finds that different victim groups are unable to acknowledge the suffering of others. Victims of the genocide in Rwanda feel little sympathy for victims of the current regime, who in turn lack empathy because their struggle is unacknowledged. The genocide victims argue that their suffering is greater. Neither group is able to transcend the damage done to its own group and to embrace the intrinsic value of human rights as such, regardless of the identity of the victims. In a bitter analogy, the logic applied by those who committed the genocide also defines the gap between the different victim organizations. The Rwandan government, which came to power as a consequence of a military victory over the groups that actively engaged in the genocide, does little to encourage reconciliation.

None of this detracts from the value of the starting point that the experiences of those who suffer human rights violations should be the main source of change in human rights at the

63

normative level. It is essential that the role of these groups in the creation of global human rights norms is increased, if human rights are to be a living instrument responsive to changing needs. But the victim perspective is not the only perspective, and the input of the interpreters, which include transnational NGO networks and enlightened individuals within the institutions which have the formal power to legislate at both domestic and international levels, is also important for reaching the best outcome.

Notes

1 UN Committee on Economic, Social and Cultural Rights, 'General Comment no. 9: The Domestic Application of the Covenant', UN doc. E/C.12/1998/24, par. 11.

2 For more information, consult <www.dhescbrasil.org>

3 European Court of Human Rights, *Colas Est v. France* (no. 37971/97), Judgment of 16 April 2002. The European Convention on Human Rights allows applications from 'any person, non-governmental organisation or group of individuals'. Companies fall within the latter category.

4 Art. I-4 of the draft EU Constitution (as adopted on 20 June 2003 by the European Convention on the Future of Europe). Human rights appear in Article I-7 under the heading 'Fundamental Rights'. The heads of state and government of the EU adopted the text on 18 June 2004.

5 F. Gianviti, 'Economic, Social and Cultural Rights and the International Monetary Fund', UN doc. E/C.12/2001/WP.5, par. 39.

6 See for an example, UN Human Rights Committee, *A Newspaper Company v. Trinidad and Tobago* (no. 360/1989), Decision of 14 July 1989.

7 UN Committee on Economic, Social and Cultural Rights, 'General Comment no. 3: The Nature of State Parties' Obligations', UN doc. E/1991/23, par. 10.

8 UN Committee on Economic, Social and Cultural Rights, 'General Comment no. 9: The Domestic Application of the Covenant', UN doc. E/C.12/1998/24, par. 10.

9 Gianviti, 'Economic, Social and Cultural Rights and the International Monetary Fund', UN doc. E/C.12/2001/WP.5, par. 24.

10 See Arts 2 and 5 of the Convention on the Elimination of All Forms of Discrimination Against Women (18 December 1979), and Arts 2 and 4 of the International Convention on the Elimination of Racial Discrimination (21 December 1965).

11 European Court of Human Rights, *Bankovic et al. v. Belgium and nine other States* (no. 52207/99), Judgment of 12 December 2001, par. 71.

12 Inter-American Commission on Human Rights, *Coard et al. v. United States* (no. 109/99), Report of 29 September 1999.

13 Inter-American Commission on Human Rights, *Detainees in Guantanamo Bay, Cuba*, request for precautionary measures (13 March 2002).

14 UN Human Rights Committee, *Lopez Burgos v. Uruguay* (no. R.12/52), Decision of 29 July 1981, par. 12.3.

15 UN Committee on Economic, Social and Cultural Rights, 'General Comment no. 11: Plans of Action for Primary Education, UN doc. E/C.12/1998/24, par. 9.

16 UN Committee on Economic, Social and Cultural Rights, 'General Comment no. 8: The Relationship between Economic Sanctions and Respect for Economic, Social and Cultural Rights', UN doc. E/C.12/1997/8, par. 7.

4 | After 9/11

After years of internal debate among its membership, in 2001 Amnesty International decided to open up its mission to some consideration of economic, social and cultural rights. It was a major step (at least on paper) that could potentially make a significant contribution to achieving *real* indivisibility of human rights. Then the attacks on the World Trade Center and the Pentagon happened.

At the time I served as the chair of a working group advising Amnesty's leadership on how to implement the decision to move into economic, social and cultural rights. Half of the working group's membership was non-Amnesty. It was fascinating work. Our stance was not to single out two or three economic, social and cultural rights (as the organization had done for civil and political rights in the past), but instead to focus on excluded or marginalized people who suffer systematic or severe deprivation of economic, social and cultural rights. The recommendation was well received.

After 9/11, however, new concerns emerged. The human rights that Amnesty had traditionally defended – the prohibition of torture, freedom of expression – were under threat. The organization was forced to dig in in the trenches to defend causes it had deemed already won. Should not all efforts be directed towards countering the unilateralism of the world's one remaining hegemonic power? On the other hand, US unilateralism in human rights was not new. US courts consistently took the *civil* rights in the American constitution and not international human rights law as their point of reference. The standard for judging the behaviour of other states had always been US society, which was held to be morally privileged. September 11 would in any case not affect the US position on economic, social and cultural rights. Its opposition to those rights would simply continue.

To Amnesty's credit, the plan to launch a major campaign on economic, social and cultural rights (along the lines suggested by the working group) was not shelved. Nevertheless, huge resources went into addressing the human rights impact of post-9/11 security measures, and in preventing long-established international human rights treaties from being swept under the carpet in the 'War against Evil'.

September 11 has not encouraged a balanced approach to human rights. Its direct impact on human rights has been negative. The problem of the selective use of human rights was illustrated by the appeal to 'human rights' made by coalition forces for the purposes of justifying the military intervention in Iraq. Finally, 9/11 and its aftermath may well have hurt human rights efforts to improve the living conditions of those marginalized by dominant political and economic forces.

The direct impact on human rights of the 11 September attacks and their aftermath

In international law, the 11 September attacks constituted a crime against humanity, as defined in the Statute of the International Criminal Court.[1] This was a large-scale massive attack aimed at civilians, consciously planned as part of a strategy to achieve political aims. The attacks were also an example of a globalized form of terrorism perpetrated by a non-state actor, and arguably planned in parts of the world far removed from the region where the attack occurred.

The large-scale use of indiscriminate violence for political purposes is in itself very worrying from a human rights perspective. Human rights seek to achieve respect for the integrity of all human life. Whatever one's misgivings about the role of the

United States in world politics and human rights, the attacks were horrendous and unjustifiable. The perpetrators were successful in attaining their immediate objectives, and were encouraged by a positive response from some circles where anti-US sentiment ran high. Other acts involving random killing, such as the March 2004 commuter train bombings in Madrid, followed. Large-scale terrorism is a regular feature of the post-9/11 world, and the damage this does to the notion that all human life deserves respect can hardly be ignored. Terrorism lowers the standard, and encourages states and other actors similarly to disregard human rights.

The introduction to the 2004 Amnesty International Annual Report offers an overview of the types of human rights violations that have occurred in the context of the state response to the 11 September attacks. The overview opens with a bleak paragraph:

> The current framework of international law and multilateral action is undergoing the most sustained attack since its establishment half a century ago. International human rights and humanitarian law is being directly challenged as ineffective in responding to the security issues of the present and the future. In the name of the 'war on terror' governments are eroding human rights principles, standards and values. The international community appears unable or unwilling to halt this trend. Armed groups, meanwhile, continue to flout their responsibilities under international humanitarian law.

The Amnesty report and others like it contain a damning critique of state practices in response to terrorism. Such practices include:

- The repackaging of existing repressive human rights practices as anti-terrorism measures.
- The use of vague definitions of terrorism in domestic legisla-

tion, combined with sweeping powers for law-enforcement officials. Such powers include a relaxation of rules on the use of phone tapping, police surveillance, use of the internet etc. The use of broad definitions of terrorism leads to the criminalization of accepted forms of dissent, as protected by the freedoms of opinion and expression.

- The tightening of immigration and asylum policies, resulting in the denial of protection to those seeking refuge from persecution by countries deemed to support terrorism, and the forcible return of persons originating from those countries even in the face of serious risk of human rights violations.
- The delivery of, or an increase in, military aid to governments deemed strategically important in the war against terrorism, even if their human rights records are poor.

In addition, serious human rights violations have been committed in the context of the armed interventions in Afghanistan and in Iraq, both of which were triggered by the 11 September events (cf. Ross 2004). Prominent violations included US detention practices at Guantanamo Bay, such as: the unlawful indefinite detention of various categories of persons who should not be in detention at all; the denial of access to a judicial body able to a review the legality of the detention; and, in cases where detainees are charged with a criminal offence, trials by military commissions falling short of international fair trial standards. In addition, in 2004, there was increasing reporting[2] of the abusive treatment of Iraqi detainees by coalition forces, most notably at the Abu Ghraib prison, a prison that had been notorious for brutality under Saddam Hussein. Torture and inhuman and degrading treatment occurred while detainees were being prepared for interviews by military intelligence teams. Credible evidence surfaced that the abusive treatment was not random but orchestrated. Private security firms were involved in the conduct of interrogations.

Box 4.1 *Joint Statement of Special Rapporteurs, UN doc. E/CN.4/2004/4 (5 August 2003), Annex 1, on Terrorism and Human Rights*

The special rapporteurs/representatives, independent experts and chairpersons of the working groups of the special procedures of the Commission on Human Rights and of the advisory services programme, meeting in Geneva from 23 to 27 June 2003, express alarm at the growing threats against human rights, threats that necessitate a renewed resolve to defend and promote these rights. They also note the impact of this environment on the effectiveness and independence of special procedures.

Although they share in the unequivocal condemnation of terrorism, they voice profound concern at the multiplication of policies, legislation and practices increasingly being adopted by many countries in the name of the fight against terrorism which affect negatively the enjoyment of virtually all human rights – civil, cultural, economic, political and social.

They draw attention to the dangers inherent in the indiscriminate use of the term 'terrorism', and the resulting new categories of discrimination. They recall that, in accordance with the International Covenant on Civil and Political Rights and pursuant to the Convention against Torture and Other Cruel, Inhuman or Degrading Treatment or Punishment, certain rights are non-derogable and that any measures of derogation from the other rights guaranteed by the Covenant must be made in strict conformity with the provisions of its article 4.

The special rapporteurs/representatives, independent experts and chairpersons of the working groups of the special procedures of the Commission and of the advisory services programme deplore the fact that, under the pretext of combating terrorism, human rights defenders are threatened and vulnerable groups are targeted and discriminated against on the basis of origin and socio-economic status, in particular migrants, refugees and asylum-seekers, indigenous peoples and people fighting for their land rights or against the negative effects of economic globalization policies.

They strongly affirm that any measures taken by States to combat terrorism must be in accordance with States' obligations under the international human rights instruments.

They are determined, in the framework of their respective mandates, to monitor and investigate developments in this area and call upon all those committed to respect for human rights, including the United Nations, to be vigilant to prevent any abuse of counter-terrorism measures.

Surely, the use of these practices by the dominant military power has a legitimizing effect. Other states faced with violent dissent must feel that they are entitled to do the same. The United States has a long tradition of indulging in human rights rhetoric in its foreign policy, in contrast to the reality of detention practices in Iraq, notwithstanding the prosecution of a number of military personnel. Again, there is a risk that the hypocrisy of the discourse will inspire others that look to the USA for guidance on how to organize the fight against terrorism.

Human rights organizations were not alone in expressing alarm. In June 2003, the Special Rapporteurs and individual experts of the UN Commission on Human Rights adopted a joint statement on terrorism and human rights.

The joint statement (see Box 4.1) confirms that a number of human rights are not subject to derogation under any circumstances.[3] These include the right to life, the right to be free from torture and other inhumane or degrading treatment or punishment, the right to be free from slavery or servitude, the right to be free from retroactive application of penal laws and the right to freedom of thought, conscience and religion. International humanitarian law explicitly guarantees the right to fair trial during armed conflict.

The Special Rapporteurs express concern about the indiscriminate use of the term 'terrorism'. It may be worth recalling that the UN General Assembly declaration on measures to eliminate terrorism[4] describes 'acts intended or calculated to provoke a state of terror in the general public, a group of persons or particular persons for political purposes' as terrorist acts. Such acts are 'in any circumstance unjustifiable, whatever the considerations of a political, philosophical, ideological, racial, ethnic, religious or any other nature that may be invoked to justify them'.

At the United Nations, the counter-terrorism committee of the UN Security Council currently coordinates anti-terrorism activities. The committee consists of all the members of the Council. It was created in September 2001, in direct response to the 9/11 attacks.[5] All UN member-states report to the committee on their implementation of anti-terrorism measures as listed by the UN Security Council. Resolution 1373 setting up the committee does not insist on the need to respect human rights in the context of anti-terrorist campaigns. Resolution 1456, however, does: 'States must ensure that any measures taken to combat terrorism comply with all their obligations under international law, and should adopt such measures in accordance with international law, in particular international human rights, refugee and humanitarian law.'[6]

The Office of the High Commissioner of Human Rights reports

that it now regularly provides information to the chair of the counter-terrorism committee on the findings of the relevant UN human rights bodies.[7]

Human rights and democracy as justification for the war against Iraq

The legitimacy of human rights suffers from their selective use. Human rights violations trigger very different responses. Human rights lose credibility as universal values around which actors upholding human dignity and social justice can rally when states take up human rights only when their national interest is at stake. It happens when the prospect of economic gain influences human rights positions. When national security interests are in play, the risk of a purely instrumental use of human rights is even higher. The reliance on human rights by the coalition forces as part of the justification for the 2003 armed intervention in Iraq offers a case in point.

British involvement in Iraq has a long history. During the First World War, Great Britain and France concluded a secret understanding, the Sykes–Picot Agreement (May 1916) on the partition of the Ottoman Empire into British and French spheres of influence. The agreement provided the basis for international administration over Palestine, but also submitted the largest part of what is now the territory of Iraq to British influence. Only the northern part (Mosul) was marked as French. In practice, however, British troops conquered the whole of the territory. The League of Nations awarded Britain a mandate over Iraq in 1920. The proclamation by the British military commander, Lieutenant General Sir Stanley Maude, shortly after he occupied Baghdad (see Box 4.2), received a great deal of attention in British newspapers at the start of the 2003 war.

In practice, the liberation of Iraq from alien institutions took some time. Iraq gained independence only in 1932 under

Box 4.2 Excerpts from the Proclamation of Baghdad, issued to the inhabitants of Baghdad on 19 March 1917 by Lieut. General Sir Stanley Maude

In the name of my King, and in the name of the peoples over whom he rules, I address you as follows:

Our military operations have as their object the defeat of the enemy, and the driving of him from these territories. In order to complete this task, I am charged with absolute and supreme control of all regions in which British troops operate; but our armies do not come into your cities and lands as conquerors or enemies, but as liberators. Since the days of Halaka your city and your lands have been subject to the tyranny of strangers, your palaces have fallen into ruins, your gardens have sunk in desolation, and your forefathers and yourselves have groaned in bondage. Your sons have been carried off to wars not of your seeking, your wealth has been stripped from you by unjust men and squandered in distant places. [...]

But you, people of Baghdad, whose commercial prosperity and whose safety from oppression and invasion must ever be a matter of the closest concern to the British Government, are not to understand that it is the wish of the British Government to impose upon you alien institutions. It is the hope of the British Government that the aspirations of your philosophers and writers shall be realised and that once again the people of Baghdad shall flourish, enjoying their wealth and substance under institutions which are in consonance with their sacred laws and their racial ideals. [...]

O people of Baghdad, remember that for 26 generations you have suffered under strange tyrants who have ever endeavoured to set one Arab house against another in order

74

> that they might profit by your dissensions. This policy is abhorrent to Great Britain and her Allies, for there can be neither peace nor prosperity where there is enmity and misgovernment. Therefore I am commanded to invite you, through your nobles and elders and representatives, to participate in the management of your civil affairs in collaboration with the political representatives of Great Britain who accompany the British Army, so that you may be united with your kinsmen in North, East, South, and West in realising the aspirations of your race.

a monarchy imposed by the British, which promptly allowed the monopoly on Iraqi oil production to continue in the hands of a consortium of Western companies. During the mandate period, Great Britain introduced a number of democratic institutions, but at the same time ensured that these institutions took decisions that were favourable to British interests. In response, Iraqi nationalism developed. Marr (2003: 8) argues that parliamentary institutions did not take root in Iraq, precisely because Britain manipulated them. 'It embedded in Iraq a strong strand of political thinking among the intelligentsia that was opposed to foreign interference – especially from the West – and distrustful of cooperation with it.'

External imposition of democracy is a lost cause. External actors may be able to create the conditions for a transition from authoritarianism to democracy, by withdrawing regime aid or by sheer superior military force, but internal factors determine the sustainability of democracy. Decolonization offers plenty of examples of colonial powers establishing democracy with their last breath. The institutions soon collapsed. They were alien and barren. Leftwich has developed the following test of conditions that need to be fulfilled if democracy is to take root in developing countries (Leftwich 1993: 615–17):

- there is no challenge of the geographical, constitutional and political legitimacy of the state
- a consensus exists about the rules of the political game
- elected governments exercise restraint in the extent of policy change
- a pluralistic civil society exists, which is sufficiently autonomous from the state
- there is no serious internal security threat by armed opposition groups
- societies are not too divided ethnically, religiously or culturally, especially when such divisions are compounded by real or perceived material inequalities
- there is no deep economic crisis sharpening existing inequality

Few such conditions are fulfilled in Iraq today, or elsewhere in the Middle East. Pinkney (2003: 207) describes the Middle East as the 'empty chair in the democratic world'. There has not been an evolutionary route to democracy in the region. Undemocratic forms of government have proven difficult to dislodge, given the wealth of their economies. Little room for autonomous social groups emerged.

The radical, immediate imposition of democracy by a foreign invader almost inevitably implies that the invader continues to wield an important veto over political decisions. That, after all, is what invasions aim to do. This logic, however, is irreconcilable with an understanding of democracy as a form of government that is responsive to the wishes of the local population. The imposition of instant democracy also means alienation of the old elite, which is not given any chance to secure at least some of its interests in the new order, leaving it only the option of seeking the reversal of the newly established regime (cf. Pinkney 2003: 179–94). In these circumstances, consolidation of democracy is a very tall order.

The position that sustainable democracy will seldom result from a transition dominated by external actors is uncontroversial. It is unlikely that the coalition forces were unaware that the chances of a sustainable democracy in the post-Saddam Hussein period were slim.

In a 2004 speech, UK Prime Minister Tony Blair acknowledged that 'however abhorrent and foul the regime and however relevant that was for the reasons I set out before the war […] regime change alone could not be and was not our justification for war. Our primary purpose was to enforce UN resolutions over Iraq and weapons of mass destruction.' Nevertheless, the importance of democratization and human rights as a justification for the war was increasingly stressed, as other justifications became less plausible. The Security Council had long debated whether it wanted an armed intervention and, notwithstanding the US/UK campaign, decided against it. On weapons of mass destruction (WMD), the evidence remained ambiguous. Human Rights Watch initially took the line that it need not take a position for or against the war, because the humanitarian rationale was 'so plainly subsidiary' to other reasons given to justify war. In 2004, however, the Human Rights Watch World Report went on record to state that the conditions had not been present in the case of Iraq to justify a humanitarian intervention. In any case, clearly, the appeal of coalition governments to democratization and human rights was aimed at securing political support for the intervention from that part of Western public opinion that was sincerely concerned about the repressive nature of the Saddam Hussein regime. In the 2004 speech (see Box 4.3), Prime Minister Blair explicitly uses the human rights argument in his defence of the war. The values of the human spirit should triumph over terrorism and

Box 4.3 Excerpts from a speech at Sedgefield justifying military action in Iraq, delivered on 5 March 2004 by UK Prime Minister Tony Blair

September 11th was for me a revelation. [...] From September 11th on, I could see the threat plainly. Here were terrorists prepared to bring about Armageddon. Here were states whose leadership cared for no one but themselves; were often cruel and tyrannical towards their own people; and who saw WMD as a means of defending themselves against any attempt external or internal to remove them and who, in their chaotic and corrupt state, were in any event porous and irresponsible with neither the will nor capability to prevent terrorists who also hated the West, from exploiting their chaos and corruption. [...]

Here is the irony. For all the fighting, this threat cannot be defeated by security means alone. Taking strong action is a necessary but insufficient condition for defeating it. Its final defeat is only assured by the triumph of the values of the human spirit.

Which brings me to the final point. It may well be that under international law as presently constituted, a regime can systematically brutalize and oppress its people and there is nothing anyone can do, when dialogue, diplomacy and even sanctions fail, unless it comes within the definition of a humanitarian catastrophe (though the 300,000 remains in mass graves already found in Iraq might be thought by some to be something of a catastrophe). This may be the law, but should it be?

We know now, if we didn't before, that our own self-interest is ultimately bound up with the fate of other nations. The doctrine of international community is no longer a vision of idealism. It is a practical recognition that just as within a country, citizens who are free, well educated and prosperous tend to be responsible, to feel solidarity with a society in which they have a stake; so do nations that are free, democratic and benefiting from economic progress, tend to be stable and solid partners in the advance of humankind. The best defence of our security lies in the spread of our values.

But we cannot advance these values except within a framework that recognizes their universality. If it is a global threat, it needs a global response, based on global rules.

The essence of a community is common rights and responsibilities. We have obligations in relation to each other. If we are threatened, we have a right to act. And we do not accept in a community that others have a right to oppress and brutalize their people. We value the freedom and dignity of the human race and each individual in it.

Containment will not work in the face of the global threat that confronts us. The terrorists have no intention of being contained. The states that proliferate or acquire WMD illegally are doing so precisely to avoid containment. Emphatically I am not saying that every situation leads to military action. But we surely have a duty and a right to prevent the threat materializing; and we surely have a responsibility to act when a nation's people are subjected to a regime such as Saddam's. Otherwise, we are powerless to fight the aggression and injustice which over time puts at risk our security and way of life.

Which brings us to how you make the rules and how you decide what is right or wrong in enforcing them. The UN Universal Declaration on Human Rights is a fine document.

But it is strange the United Nations is so reluctant to enforce them.

I understand the worry the international community has over Iraq. It worries that the US and its allies will by sheer force of their military might, do whatever they want, unilaterally and without recourse to any rule-based code or doctrine. But our worry is that if the UN – because of a political disagreement in its Councils – is paralysed, then a threat we believe is real will go unchallenged. [...]

This agenda must be robust in tackling the security threat that this Islamic extremism poses; and fair to all peoples by promoting their human rights, wherever they are. It means tackling poverty in Africa and justice in Palestine as well as being utterly resolute in opposition to terrorism as a way of achieving political goals. It means an entirely different, more just and more modern view of self-interest.

It means reforming the United Nations so its Security Council represents 21st-century reality; and giving the UN the capability to act effectively as well as debate. It means getting the UN to understand that, faced with the threats we have, we should do all we can to spread the values of freedom, democracy, the rule of law, religious tolerance and justice for the oppressed, however painful for some nations that may be; but that at the same time, we wage war relentlessly on those who would exploit racial and religious division to bring catastrophe to the world.

authoritarian government. In a globalized world, 'the best defence of our security lies in the spread of our values'. These values include human rights. It is in Britain's interest that human rights are respected elsewhere, because societies that respect human rights do not pose a threat. In a global community, Britain has a right to act when governments brutally oppress their peoples, and in some cases, the right to use military force, even when the United Nations declines to give authorization.

The speech offers an interesting example of how Western governments appropriate human rights, and in the process alienate the rest of the world. Human rights are 'our' values that global institutions need to promote and governments elsewhere need to respect, in order to guarantee our own security. The human rights project seeks to ensure that everyone else shares Western values, which at least implicitly are deemed superior, and supposedly do not include using dogs to attack naked prisoners.

Interestingly, the speech posits that a global community exists 'with common rights and responsibilities', but does so to construct the unilateral right of Britain to ignore the UN Security Council in order to intervene militarily to stop repression elsewhere. That determination, the speech argues, ultimately rests with Britain itself. Or perhaps with an Atlantic alliance supported by like-minded countries. The existence of a global community does not mean that industrialized countries should adhere to global rules, should take into account the views of non-Western states on human rights, or should take the right to development seriously. It means that the West has the right to intervene on foreign soil in order to defend self-defined values that it feels should be respected globally. The result is a groundswell of disaffection in communities excluded by the discourse.

Ultimately, the Blair position makes human rights subservient to Western security interests. No other explanation of the different approach to human rights violations in Iraq and in Palestine makes sense. Arab populations are acutely aware of the differentiation, and consequently greet human rights talk with increasing cynicism. The UN 'reluctance' to enforce human rights can be explained at least in part by the UN's reluctance simply to serve a Western security agenda. After all, that security agenda paved the way for a new wave of human rights violations in the context of anti-terrorism measures.

In a thoughtful report, the International Council on Human Rights Policy (ICHRP 2002) urges human rights organizations to insist on careful regard for human rights law, and on the need to defend precise legal language in a context where emotions provoked by terrorism run high. On the other hand, the report also argues that human rights organizations must take account of causes and motives (ibid., p. 47), i.e. the flagrant inequity of the world in which we live:

> From this wider perspective, human rights organisations exist to bring justice and promote human dignity. They cannot stand aside from these larger issues or take refuge from them in the decipherment of technical legal rules. They must be seen to be engaged, publicly in the defence of large human interests – and eventually, the laws they stand up for must also be seen to defend those larger interests too.

Consequently, the report advocates alliances between human rights organizations and social movements including the anti-globalization campaigns. Such alliances: 'Offer opportunities to step out of sometimes narrow preoccupations and disciplines, to join other organisations around broad issues such as social exclusion, and to build support for human rights in new constituencies.' The alliances are a necessary antidote to the partisan use governments make of human rights in the fight against terrorism.

Postponing global social justice?

In Resolution 1456, the UN Security Council emphasizes:

> that continuing international efforts to enhance dialogue and broaden the understanding among civilizations, in an effort to

prevent the indiscriminate targeting of different religions and cultures, to further strengthen the campaign against terrorism, and to address unresolved regional conflicts and the full range of global issues, including development issues, will contribute to international cooperation and collaboration, which by themselves are necessary to sustain the broadest possible fight against terrorism.[8]

The Security Council recognizes the importance of international development cooperation in combating terrorism. International development cooperation is also important from the perspective of human rights, because – at least potentially – aid makes additional resources available for the realization of human rights in countries where resources are scarce.

In September 2000 – a year before the 9/11 attacks – the UN General Assembly, at its Millennium Summit, adopted a declaration[9] laying down the 'Millennium Development Goals'. The Millennium Declaration is an attempt by the United Nations to achieve coherence among the development policies of both donor and recipient countries. The aim of the declaration is to direct development efforts of all relevant actors towards the realization of agreed goals. Some of the targets are specific and have to be met within a specific time. UNDP has described the declaration as a compact among nations to end human poverty.[10] The text includes a section on human rights, although the goals and targets are not formulated in human rights language. Examples include commitments to halve between 1990 and 2015 the proportion of people who suffer from hunger, to achieve universal primary education by 2015, to eliminate gender disparity in education and to reduce child mortality rates. Although the declaration is non-binding, it serves as a yardstick for evaluating the development efforts of both donor and recipient countries. Countries are not legally obliged to implement the goals, but stand to be criticized if they do not, and to be rewarded (e.g. through international assistance) when they do. Although the Millennium Declaration includes a chapter on peace and security that calls for concerted action against international terrorism, the goals themselves are poverty-orientated and not security-orientated.

Arguably, the Millennium Declaration is the closest the international community has come to organizing international solidarity for achieving a number of human-rights-related goals. As explained earlier, the human rights system itself is based on the distribution of responsibility, not solidarity. Obviously, one can also read the declaration cynically. The right to primary education is an immediately applicable right in the International Covenant on Economic, Social and Cultural Rights, while the declaration perceives of its achievement in 2015 as a mere target. But at least the declaration recognizes that an international effort by various actors will be required if even very basic levels of satisfaction of economic, social and cultural rights are to be achieved within the next decade.

The declaration was, however, adopted in the pre-9/11 world. The concern today is that developed countries are redirecting resources originally intended for human-rights-related goals towards the fight against terrorism in developing countries. The perceived self-interest of developed states is the primary motive for such a shift.

The venue where this battle is being fought is the Development Assistance Committee (DAC) of the Organisation for Economic Co-operation and Development (OECD). The Development Assistance Committee brings together the major donors of development aid. It also provides statistics and evaluations of the development policies of the different members. In order to perform this function, the committee has adopted a definition of the type of measures that are eligible as official development assistance (see Box 4.4): development aid is at least 25 per cent grant, has the promotion of economic development or welfare

> ### Box 4.4 *Official Development Assistance (ODA) as defined by the Development Assistance Committee of the Organization for Economic Cooperation and Development*
>
> Official development assistance is defined as those flows to countries on Part I of the DAC List and to multilateral institutions for flows to Part I aid recipients which are: provided by official agencies, including state and local governments, or by their executive agencies; and transaction of which: is administered with the promotion of the economic development and welfare of developing countries as its main objective; and is concessional in character and conveys a grant element of at least 25 per cent (calculated at a rate of discount of 10 per cent).

as its main objective and goes to developing countries. Substantially, OECD donors use the Millennium Development Goals as a yardstick for evaluating individual country performance.

The OECD definition does not include international cooperation for security. Some OECD member-states would like to see a change that would enable them to count money made available to developing countries for combating terrorism as development aid. This would not necessarily mean that the resources flowing to developing countries would increase. On the contrary, it may well imply that parts of current donor budgets would no longer be available for human-rights-related development aid. Chances that the Millennium Development Goals are met – predictions are not optimistic – decrease accordingly.

In response to pressure, the OECD Development Assistance Committee produced two papers which both include a policy statement adopted by DAC members. In *A Development Co-*

operation Lens on Terrorism Prevention,[11] the committee recognizes that in order to make development cooperation more effective in combating support for terrorism, there may be 'implications for priorities including budget allocations and levels and definitions of ODA eligibility criteria'.[12] The paper also states, however, that aid budgets may need to increase accordingly, and that development aid should not become an instrument of non-development interests.[13]

The paper acknowledges the problem of increased development aid to states that commit human rights violations. OECD countries may be tempted to overlook abuses taking place because they need cooperation from that relevant country's government. This is an area, the paper states, where consistency needs to improve. The risk is obvious. Perhaps the authors had in mind the EU's enthusiasm for embracing Pakistan as a partner country. EU development aid to Pakistan has significantly increased since 9/11, culminating in the conclusion of an expanded EU–Pakistan cooperation agreement on 29 April 2004.

Support for the introduction of anti-terrorism measures or legislation may well lead to a curtailment of human rights (e.g. restrictions on media freedom), particularly if the recipient governments have dubious human rights records.

According to the paper:

Another potential area for policy incoherence can be noted in relation to short-term security and political exigencies in the campaign to eradicate terrorism. Balancing security and freedom carries risks. Western governments fighting terrorism must carefully avoid behaviours that restrict liberties to an extent that impedes democracy and the rule of law and reinforces the negative image that terrorists try to promote.[14]

Roughly the same line of thinking runs through a second recent DAC paper, *Security System Reform and Governance*.[15]

Again, the paper emphasizes that support for security system reform – defined as aid seeking to increase the ability of partner countries to meet the range of security needs within their societies in a manner consistent with democratic norms and sound principles of governance and the rule of law – may need to draw on resources other than those recognized by DAC as official development assistance: 'In this connection, it is also important to develop whole-of-government responses to ensure that assistance needs are met from a combination of relevant budget sources, and that the integrity and the credibility of the DAC statistics are preserved and development funds are not misused.'[16]

The paper warns that pooled funding arrangements may enable other departments to tap into development assistance. There is a risk that traditional security-related programmes are simply relabelled as development aid, and then claimed from that budget.

An annex to the paper on the current practice of both donor and recipient countries confirms that the risk is real. A significant amount of activity in the security domain is underway. A number of OECD countries are promoting reforms of security systems under the heading of the 'war on terrorism', intended to bolster the intelligence and security capacity of partner states: 'This is occasioning significant trade-offs between the initial emphasis on strengthening operational effectiveness and the longer-term goal of improving transparency and accountability in the security system.'[17] In other words, aid does not go into ensuring that security systems respect civil and political rights, but into security systems as such. The discussion on the definition of official development assistance eligibility will continue. Further proposals for change are expected in 2005.

In a recent document, the non-governmental Reality of Aid network convincingly argues that there is little synergy between a rights-based strategy to promote peace and social justice, and strategies to combat terrorism:

> The former emphasise the creation of viable and broadly responsive state and civil institutions, the promotion of social cohesion based on justice, and tackling the backdrop of socio-economic conditions that underlie endemic poverty and exclusion. In contrast current actions by governments (North and South) to prevent and counter terrorism are oriented to the restriction of people's rights, deepening repression of communities in conflict with their government (whether peaceful or otherwise), strengthening within government the military/the police/agencies for covert action and the creation of a climate of fear among citizens. These pro-active anti-terrorism measures do little to nourish climates for peace and development in the interests of people living in poverty.[18]

In summary, the 9/11 events and their aftermath have not led to an increased interest in the realization of the human rights of marginalized communities in developing countries. On the contrary, the dominant perception of these communities is that they constitute a bedrock for international terrorism. The countries targeted by international terrorism and the home governments of the communities share the same view. The response of the governmental actors primarily focuses on the strengthening of security systems. There are few signs of dialogue, let alone of increased investment in living conditions.

Assistance to these communities is essential if the trend is to be reversed. Human rights can support the reversal of the trend, not only by insisting that any anti-terrorism measure needs to conform to international human rights law, but also by operating as an instrument of social mobilization. The global human rights movement and institutions should be instrumental in opening up a political space where the claims of marginalized communities can be heard.

Notes

1 Art. 7, Statute of the International Criminal Court, 17 July 1998.

2 See for instance S. M. Hersh (2004), 'Chain of Command', *New Yorker*, 17 May 2004.

3 Cf. Art. 4, International Covenant on Civil and Political Rights (16 December 1966).

4 UN General Assembly Resolution 49/60 (9 December 1994), annex.

5 UN Security Council Resolution 1373 (28 September 2001).

6 UN Security Council Resolution 1456 (20 January 2003), par. 6.

7 UN doc. E/CN.4/2004/91 (12 March 2004), par. 9.

8 UN Security Council Resolution 1456 (20 January 2003), par. 10.

9 UN General Assembly Resolution 55/2 (8 September 2000).

10 The 2003 UNDP *Human Development Report* focuses on the Millennium Development Goals. See UNDP, *Human Development Report 2003* (Oxford: Oxford University Press, 2003).

11 OECD, *A Development Co-operation Lens on Terrorism Prevention* (Paris: OECD, 2003).

12 Ibid., p. 11.

13 Ibid., p. 8.

14 Ibid., p. 19.

15 OECD, *Security System Reform and Governance* (Paris: OECD, 2004).

16 Ibid., p. 20.

17 Ibid., p. 50.

18 The Reality of Aid Networks (2004), *Governance: Reclaiming the Concept from a Human Rights Perspective* (2004), p. 18. Available from the Reality of Aid website <www.realityofaid.org>

5 | Geneva

Geneva is an unlikely city to be the human rights capital of the world. Behold, a city of splendour, of lakes and parks, of ostentatious wealth and tedious Swiss souvenirs, far removed from the deprivation of human rights abuse. People lounging on the Quai du Mont-Blanc are passing through. They are here, but will be elsewhere soon. Suitcases wait in their rooms, filled with running shorts or burkhas. Geneva is a globalized city. Home to many international institutions, a financial centre and a transport node. According to 2003 figures, the 'pearl of the lake' ranks eighth on the list of most expensive cities in the world. Extreme poverty is discussed in air-conditioned rooms where dress codes rule, where access is by badge provided upon due fulfilment of administrative requirements, and where people pretend to stop time for the sake of extending meetings. At night exhausted delegates assemble in restaurants and at cocktail parties, enjoying the taste of privilege. In Geneva, the heroes are diplomats.

The Geneva-based UN human rights system is both an obstacle and an opportunity for adjusting human rights to the challenge of economic globalization. Insiders are convinced of its relevance. Outsiders much less so. One of the few collections of essays devoted to the theme of globalization and human rights (Brysk 2002) simply ignores the Geneva system. If the book is correct in its assessment, there is reason for concern. It is difficult to imagine how one could develop a human rights response to globalization without some reliance on global human rights institutions.

In substance, a human rights response to economic globalization needs to come to grips with the responsibility of actors other than the state, which is primarily responsible. These actors include economically dominant states that impact on other economies as a consequence of the lowering of economic barriers, companies that organize across boundaries, and influential economic and financial intergovernmental organizations. The central issue discussed here is whether the Geneva system has been able to respond to the challenge.

Certainly, a number of initiatives have been taken. For years, the UN Commission on Human Rights has endeavoured to clarify the scope of the right to development as a mechanism for sharing human rights responsibility among all the actors in the international community. Various parts of the Geneva system engage in a dialogue with the international financial institutions. In 2003, the sub-commission on the promotion and protection of human rights launched a new set of norms on the responsibilities of transnational corporations and other business enterprises with regard to human rights.

None of these initiatives necessarily affects the life of those marginalized by states and markets. The ultimate test is whether the people on the Quai du Mont-Blanc are able to connect to others whom they may never meet, but for whom human rights violations are a fact of everyday life.

The contribution of the UN human rights system

A usual distinction within the UN human rights system is between treaty bodies and charter-based bodies. The office of UN High Commissioner of Human Rights constitutes the third pole. The institutional maze is not very appealing. The United Nations has a tendency to respond to new problems by adding new institutions, and so the organizational structure of the UN human rights institutions has gradually developed into a labyrinth. On the other hand, little sense can be made of the

Geneva

outcomes the system produces without some insight into the organizational set-up. Figure 5.1 shows an official map produced by the UN itself.

The committees consist of individual experts who ideally take human rights seriously and disregard the foreign policy of their country of origin. They monitor state compliance with a specific human rights treaty. Each major human rights treaty has its own monitoring body composed of independent experts: the Human

---

Box 5.1 *Human rights in the United Nations system (see also Figure 5.1)*

UN specialized agencies and other bodies with some concern for, and responsibilities in the area of, human rights

- International Labour Organization (ILO): trade union rights, child labour, bonded labour, and labour rights generally.
- UN Educational, Scientific and Cultural Organization (UNESCO): the right to education, human rights education.
- World Health Organization (WHO): the right to healthcare, including for HIV/AIDS.
- UN Development Programme (UNDP): the right to development.
- Food and Agricultural Organization (FAO): the right to food.
- UN Children's Fund (UNICEF): the rights of the child.
- UN High Commissioner for Refugees (UNHCR): the rights of refugees and displaced persons.
- Bretton Woods institutions, including the World Bank and the International Monetary Fund (IMF): to do human rights impact assessments.

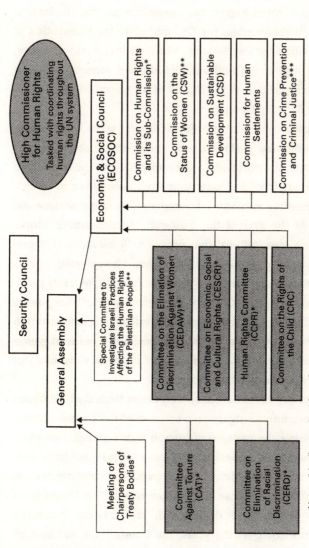

Figure 5.1 **Human rights in the United Nations system (provided by the UN High Commissioner for Human Rights). This chart is intended to be illustrative, not definitive.**

Notes: * bodies serviced from Geneva ** bodies serviced from New York *** bodies serviced from Vienna

High Commissioner for Human Rights
Tasked with coordinating human rights throughout the UN system

Economic & Social Council (ECOSOC)

Commission on Human Rights and its Sub-Commission*

Commission on the Status of Women (CSW)**

Commission on Sustainable Development (CSD)

Commission for Human Settlements

Commission on Crime Prevention and Criminal Justice***

Security Council

General Assembly

Special Committee to Investigate Israeli Practices Affecting the Human Rights of the Palestinian People**

Committee on the Elimination of Discrimination Against Women (CEDAW)**

Committee on Economic, Social and Cultural Rights (CESCR)*

Human Rights Committee (CCPR)*

Committee on the Rights of the Child (CRC)

Meeting of Chairpersons of Treaty Bodies*

Committee Against Torture (CAT)*

Committee on Elimination of Racial Discrimination (CERD)*

Rights Committee (monitoring the International Covenant on Civil and Political Rights), the UN Committee on Economic, Social and Cultural Rights, the Committee on the Elimination of Racial Discrimination, the Committee on the Elimination of Discrimination Against Women, the Committee Against Torture, the Committee on the Rights of the Child and, recently, the Committee on Protection of the Rights of All Migrant Workers and Members of Their Families.

The various committees enjoy different powers. All examine reports submitted periodically by state parties. States submit their reports in writing, and then appear before the committee to answer orally critical questions from committee members. Some committee members rely extensively on non-governmental sources. At the end of the dialogue, the committee adopts 'concluding observations' that occasionally establish that certain state practices violate human rights. The committees also adopt general comments clarifying the meaning of treaty provisions, and hold discussion days on topical issues. Other powers attributed to (some of) the committees include the consideration of complaints by states and individuals, and the investigation at the committee's proper initiative of systemic violations (for details see Nowak 2003: 78–104).

The Charter-based bodies broadly derive from the UN Charter that defines human rights as a concern of the United Nations and envisages the creation of human rights bodies. The main body is the UN Commission on Human Rights – not to be confused, as newspapers perennially do, with the similarly named, but very different Human Rights Committee. The Commission is *the* UN political body dealing with human rights. It consists of governments. Over the years, the Commission has created numerous thematic and country special procedures, involving the appointment of working groups, Special Rapporteurs and the like, many of whom are encountered in the remainder of this chapter. The sub-commission on the promotion and protection of human rights, consisting of experts sitting in their individual capacity, assists the Commission in its work.

The High Commissioner for Human Rights is the principal UN official with responsibility for human rights. The World Conference on Human Rights created the post in 1993 (see Nowak 2003: 133–4). The office of the High Commissioner provides administrative and substantive support to the treaty-monitoring bodies and the Charter-based bodies, but the institution also has the more substantial tasks of supporting human rights at the domestic level, and of mainstreaming human rights throughout the whole of the United Nations system. Geneva is far from New York, where the UN's high politics takes place. The physical distance obliges people to commute. The human rights mood that prevails in Geneva may not travel well to New York, where security is of the highest concern. In addition, mainstreaming is still a necessity in the UN specialized agencies as well. As Box 5.1 indicates, they may have 'some concern' for human rights, but not necessarily consistent policies.

Treaty bodies As a body that monitors treaty obligations in the area of civil and political rights, the Human Rights Committee tends to focus on human rights violations perpetrated by governments that abuse state powers or fail to provide safety. The impact of globalization on civil and political rights – as felt in the expansion of cross-border crime, the consequences of migration, the privatization of law and order services – has received little attention, as the committee clings to a fairly strict focus on the responsibility of each separate state under the treaty. Occasionally, the committee does specify that the state needs to regulate the behaviour of other actors (e.g. when prison services are contracted out), or that there is a cross-boundary dimension to a human rights problem under review, but there is no

95

Box 5.2 *UN Human Rights Committee,* Ominayak v. Canada *(no. 167/1984), decision of 26 March 1990*

In 1984, Chief Bernard Ominayak, the elected chief of the Lubicon Lake band, a Cree Indian band living in the Canadian Province of Alberta, alleged a breach of the right to self-determination in Article 1 of the ICCPR by the Canadian government. The provincial government of Alberta had been allowed to expropriate territory claimed by the Lubicon Lake band for the benefit of private corporate interests by granting leases for oil and gas development. It was alleged that the destruction of the natural environment had deprived the band of its traditional means of subsistence. Six years later, the committee found that it could not address the claim on the right to self-determination, for procedural reasons. Under the Optional Protocol, the committee could only decide communications by individuals claiming a violation of their individual rights. The right to self-determination was a collective right, and therefore outside the committee's jurisdiction under the Optional Protocol. The committee did, however, find that many of the claims presented raised issues under Article 27, ICCPR, which protects the rights of 'persons belonging to minorities'. The committee found that: 'Historical inequities, to which the state party refers, and certain more recent developments threaten the way of life and culture of the Lubicon Lake Band, and constitute a violation of article 27 so long as they continue' (par. 33). However, the compensation already offered by the Canadian government in the course of the domestic negotiation process, i.e. the reservation of an area of land and an amount of money, was deemed sufficient as a remedy. The band could therefore not stop the corporate exploitation of its territory.

systematic attention paid to the impact of globalization on civil and political rights.

States that ratify the First Optional Protocol to the International Covenant on Civil and Political Rights allow the Human Rights Committee to hear individual complaints. The case law of the committee is generally of interest, but of little relevance to globalization issues. In the few cases that are substantively relevant, the committee's decisions (which are recommendatory in nature) do not break new ground.

The Ominayak decision (see Box 5.2) shows the inherent limits of the individual complaints procedure. The procedure is state-orientated and thus precludes any discussion of corporate responsibility. A claim based on a collective right to economic self-determination by an indigenous people leads to a finding of a violation of a cultural right of an individual member of a minority. Compensation is an adequate remedy. The decision does not specify what economic activities violated Article 27, and therefore offers no protection against continued commercial exploitation of the area. In a letter to the committee, dated 18 December 1991, Chief Ominayak charged that 'the imprecise wording' of the committee's decision had enabled the Canadian government publicly to invoke the decision as a justification for the subsequent selling of timber rights to a Japanese forestry company in the contested area.

Individuals do not have access to the Committee on Economic, Social and Cultural Rights. Talks at the UN Commission on Human Rights on the establishment of an individual complaints procedure have moved from an ineffective independent expert to an ominously entitled working group 'with a view to considering options relating to the elaboration of an optional protocol'.[1]

The Committee on Economic, Social and Cultural Rights held a day of general discussion on the impact of globalization on human rights in 1998. Nevertheless, Sepulveda notes the limited range of specialities within the body. The large majority of the committee's members are lawyers, while 'the supervision of the Covenant requires expertise in a variety of fields, including public health, macroeconomic policies, education, housing and so forth' (Sepulveda 2003: 94). The committee is certainly aware of the need to tackle globalization, but as its dialogue with governments demonstrates, it lacks the capacity to go much beyond identifying the issues, and raising questions at a level of some generality. Former committee member Paul Hunt has, for instance, suggested that the UN Committee on ESC rights would be well advised to analyse the country information held by the World Bank and the IMF (Hunt 2003: 153–4), but admits that the committee lacks the institutional capacity to do so.

In its concluding observations on state reports, the committee regularly refers to the process of transition to a market-orientated economy'[2] or to certain aspects of the structural adjustment programmes and economic liberalization policies[3] as 'factors and difficulties impeding the implementation of the Covenant'. Developed states, as members of international organizations, are encouraged to ensure that the policies and decisions of those organizations are in conformity with the obligations of the state parties under the Covenant.[4] Likewise, borrower countries are *strongly* recommended to take into account their obligations under the Covenant in negotiations with the international financial institutions, in order to ensure that the enjoyment of ESC rights, particularly by the most disadvantaged and marginalized groups, is not undermined.[5]

The committee has adopted a number of 'statements' clarifying the human rights approach to subjects such as intellectual property rights and the Millennium Development Goals, or encouraging WTO ministerial conferences to take human rights seriously. The 'Statement on Poverty' is a fine clarification of the rights approach to poverty.[6] The 'statements' are interesting, because they enable the committee to respond to developments in the globalization debate, and to bring together the best of what the Covenant as a whole has to offer on a globalization issue. Nothing prevents the Human Rights Committee from doing the same.

Recent general comments on the right to adequate food (1999), the right to education (1999), the right to the highest attainable standard of health (2000) and the right to water (2002) all contain specific paragraphs on the implications of globalization for the realization of these specific rights. 'General Comment no. 15' on the right to water (see Box 5.3) deals extensively with the impact of globalization on access to water.[7]

According to 'General Comment no. 15', water is primarily a social and cultural good, and not a mere economic commodity. Water, and water facilities and services, must be affordable to all. States should ensure that investments do not disproportionately favour expensive water supply services and facilities but should rather invest in services and facilities that benefit a far larger part of the population. Any payment for water services has to be based on the principle of equity, ensuring that these services, whether privately or publicly provided, are affordable for all, including socially disadvantaged groups. Discriminatory or unaffordable increases in the price of water are a violation of the Covenant. Private operators should be prevented from interfering with the enjoyment of the right to water:

Where water services (such as piped water networks, water tankers, access to rivers and wells) are operated or controlled by third parties, states parties must prevent them from compromising equal, affordable, and physical access to sufficient, safe and acceptable water. To prevent such abuses an effective regulatory system must be established, in conformity with the Covenant

Geneva

99

Box 5.3   UN Committee on Economic, Social and Cultural Rights, 'General Comment no. 15 on the Right to Water', UN doc. E/C.12/2002/11 (20 January 2003), par. 60, on obligations of actors other than states

United Nations agencies and other international organizations concerned with water, such as WHO, FAO, UNICEF, UNEP, UN-Habitat, ILO, UNDP, the International Fund for Agricultural Development (IFAD), as well as international organizations concerned with trade such as the World Trade Organization (WTO), should cooperate effectively with States parties, building on their respective expertise, in relation to the implementation of the right to water at the national level. The international financial institutions, notably the International Monetary Fund and the World Bank, should take into account the right to water in their lending policies, credit agreements, structural adjustment programmes and other development projects (see General Comment No. 2 1990), so that the enjoyment of the right to water is promoted. When examining the reports of States parties and their ability to meet the obligations to realize the right to water, the Committee will consider the effects of the assistance provided by all other actors. The incorporation of human rights law and principles in the programmes and policies by international organizations will greatly facilitate implementation of the right to water. The role of the International Federation of the Red Cross and Red Crescent Societies, International Committee of the Red Cross, the Office of the United Nations High Commissioner for Refugees (UNHCR), WHO and UNICEF, as well as non-governmental organizations and other associations, is of particular importance in relation to disaster relief and humanitarian assistance in times of emergencies. Pri-

> ority in the provision of aid, distribution and management
> of water and water facilities should be given to the most
> vulnerable or marginalized groups of the population.

and this General Comment, which includes independent
monitoring, genuine public participation and imposition of
penalties for non-compliance.[8]

States also have responsibilities beyond their own borders. Any
activity undertaken within one state should not deprive another
of its ability to realize the right. States have a duty to take steps
to prevent their own citizens and companies from violating the
right to water of individuals and communities in other countries.
Agreements concerning trade liberalization should not curtail or
inhibit a country's capacity to ensure the full realization of the
right to water, nor should the lending policies and credit agreements of the international financial institutions. A failure to take
into account the right to water when entering into agreements
with other states or with international organizations amounts
to a violation of the Covenant. These organizations also have
direct human rights responsibilities, although the committee's
internal division on the issue (Hunt 2003: 143) prevents it from
using precise wording.

Like its predecessors, 'General Comment no. 15' is a significant contribution to the development of a human rights response
to globalization, particularly because it emanates from a treaty
body, i.e. a body in principle more rigidly tied to the letter of
a treaty than the Charter bodies. Through interpretation, the
committee constructs obligations that are not explicitly provided
for in the Covenant, and were probably never imagined by its
drafters. In the case of 'General Comment no. 15', even the *right*

Geneva

Box 5.4 UN Committee on the Rights of the Child, 'The Private Sector as Service Provider and Its Role in Implementing Child Rights' (20 September 2002), par. 16 on Recommendations to Non-state Service Providers on Self-regulation

The Committee encourages non-state service providers to ensure that service provision is carried out in accordance with international standards, especially the Convention. It further encourages non-state service providers to develop self-regulation mechanisms, which would include a system of checks and balances. To that end, the Committee recommends that when developing self-regulation mechanisms, the following criteria be included in the process:

- The adoption of a Code of Ethics, or similar document, which should reflect the Convention and should be developed collectively amongst the various stakeholders and in which the four general principles of the Convention should figure prominently.
- The establishment of a system for monitoring the implementation of such code of ethics, if possible by independent experts, as well as the development of a system of transparent reporting.
- The development of indicators/benchmarks as a prerequisite for measuring progress and establishing accountability.
- The inclusion of a system enabling various partners to challenge each other regarding their respective performance in implementing the Code.
- The development of an effective complaints mechanism, to render self-regulation more accountable, including to beneficiaries, particularly in light of the general principle

> stipulating the right of the child to express his or her views freely, and have those views be given due weight in accordance with the age and maturity of the child (art. 12).

to water does not explicitly appear in the treaty. Clearly, the committee adopted the general comment in order to have a say in the ongoing international debate on water, and to prevent the adoption of regulation inspired by economics only.

Through the adoption of general comments, the committees informally update the content of treaty provisions – a simpler exercise than an outright amendment of the text. Usually, the drafting of a general comment takes months or even years, and so there is an opportunity for outside contributions to the drafts.

In 2002, the UN Committee on the Rights of the Child held a general day of discussion on the private sector that was taken to include both for-profit and not-for-profit organizations. Private service providers were called upon to respect the four general principles of non-discrimination: the best interests of the child, the right to life, survival and development, and child participation. They should engage in a continuing process of dialogue and consultation with the communities they serve and other stakeholders in order to enhance transparency and accountability.[9] The committee took a favourable view of self-regulation by private actors, but also defined minimum requirements that any self-regulation venture would need to satisfy.

Charter-based bodies The Charter-based human rights bodies take hundreds of initiatives each year. Academic lives can be spent tracking them. At the Commission on Human Rights, debates on the relationship between globalization and human

Box 5.5 UN Commission on Human Rights/Sub-Commission on the Promotion and Protection of Human Rights: Selected List of Current (2003–2004) Mechanisms Pertaining Specifically to Aspects of Globalization and Human Rights

- Commission working group on structural adjustment
- Independent expert on the effects of structural adjustment policies and foreign debt on the full enjoyment of human rights, Bernards Andrew Nyamwaya Mudho
- Commission working group on the right to development
- Independent expert on the right to development, Arjun Sengupta
- Special Rapporteur on adverse effects of the illicit movement and dumping of toxic and dangerous products and wastes on the enjoyment of human rights, Fatma-Zohra Ouhachi-Vesely
- Special Rapporteur on the sale of children, child prostitution and child pornography, Juan Miguel Petit
- Special Rapporteur on the human rights of migrants, Gabriela Rodriguez Pizarro
- Special Rapporteur on the rights of non-citizens, David Weissbrodt
- Sub-commission working group on contemporary forms of slavery
- Sub-commission working group on working methods and activities of transnational corporations
- Sub-commission working group on the Social Forum
- Special Rapporteurs on globalization and its impact on human rights, Joseph Oloka-Onyango and Deepika Udagama (completed 2003)

rights cause rifts between developing and developed states. For developed states, globalization talk is a device used by developing countries to evade responsibility for human rights violations committed at home. Globalization initiatives drain money that could otherwise be used for investigating and remedying serious human rights violations. They are not always wrong. Developing countries command a voting majority in the Commission, however, and so ample initiatives on globalization and human rights are taken. Some of the most pertinent ones are listed in Box 5.5.

In 2000, the sub-commission took the initiative to appoint two Special Rapporteurs to study the impact of globalization on the enjoyment of human rights. Joseph Oloka-Onyango (from Uganda) and Deepika Udagama (from Sri Lanka) submitted their final report in June 2003.[10] The report discusses the impact of 9/11, the tension between intellectual property rights and access to essential drugs, and developments within the international financial institutions.

Each year, the Commission on Human Rights produces a resolution on globalization that dutifully takes note of all relevant studies, and endorses or ignores their recommendations. The Commission also makes resolutions without the benefit of a preliminary study. They deal with the 'promotion of a democratic and equitable international order' or 'human rights and unilateral coercive measures'. All are debated, adopted, remain unimplemented, and are recycled in the next session. This nicely phrased paragraph from the 2003 resolution on globalization deserves a better fate: 'Globalization should be guided by the fundamental principles that underpin the corpus of human rights, such as equality, participation, accountability, non-discrimination, at both the national and international levels, respect for diversity and international cooperation and solidarity.'[11]

The various Special Rapporteurs on economic, social and

cultural rights all deal with the impact of globalization in their annual reports to the Commission, in varying depth.

They also go on missions to countries. The missions are important because they raise the profile of human rights concerns in the relevant country. They allow the assembling of first-hand information that would otherwise remain invisible at the global level.

The mission of the Special Rapporteur on adequate housing to Romania offers an interesting example. In January 2002, Miloon Kothari (from India) spent six days in Bucharest. Unforeseen (and unspecified) circumstances prevented him from visiting Romania's rural areas where the housing situation is much worse than in the capital.

The report[12] examines the state of the right to housing against the backdrop of the ongoing transition to a market-orientated economy. During communist rule, forced migration from the countryside to urban areas coincided with large-scale housing programmes led by the state. After the collapse of the regime, construction of housing by the state was virtually halted, and

---

Box 5.6 UN Commission on Human Rights: 2003 Special Rapporteurs on Economic, Social and Cultural Rights

- Special Rapporteur on the highest attainable standard of physical and mental health, Paul Hunt
- Special Rapporteur on the Right to Adequate Housing, Miloon Kothari
- Special Rapporteur on Extreme Poverty, Anne-Marie Lizi n
- Special Rapporteur on the Right to Education, Katarina Tomasevski (resigned 2004); Vernor Muñoz Villalobos
- Special Rapporteur on the Right to Food, Jean Ziegler

the housing stock was privatized. The housing stock in private hands grew from 67 per cent in 1990 to 95 per cent in 2000. Tenants became owners. They were ill prepared for the financial burden of maintenance costs. Municipal companies that used to be responsible for maintenance and repairs dissolved. New owners' associations were intended to fill the gap, but took off slowly. In addition, public utilities infrastructure started to disintegrate, resulting in high costs for water and heating. The report offers a number of cases that bring the general analysis to life, and create some sense of the reality of living conditions in Bucharest.

The Special Rapporteur concludes that: 'In the housing sector, the main focus of the Government has been to create a functioning market for housing, but at the same time, the human rights obligations stipulate the duty of Government to take immediate steps towards meeting the needs of the poor and vulnerable population who otherwise are unable to reach the benefits of the market economy.'[13] The report also highlights good practices, and suggests that these can serve as examples for other countries with economies in transition.

The Geneva system can play a useful role in identifying both global causes of human rights violations, and in suggesting adequate defences. Dominant economic actors offer privatization as a global recipe for economic growth. As a result, privatization simultaneously affects human rights in many countries. If the strategy proves to be harmful for human rights in certain circumstances, clearly change will not only need to come at the national level, but also at the level of the economic actors that are pushing the strategy globally. Ideally, the Geneva system can serve as a centre where data on the impact of privatization on human rights can be collected through country research, processed, and used for the development of global strategies. The results of the process can then be made available to all relevant actors, including to donors offering assistance to privatization from a purely economic perspective.

The Special Rapporteur on the illicit dumping of toxic waste has taken a special interest in the issue of corporate responsibility. While on mission in the United Kingdom, she reviewed court cases brought by overseas victims of multinational corporations. She noted the difficulties encountered in bringing the enterprises to justice and the fact that numerous cases were settled out of court. She was concerned about the low level of penalties 'which infringes the rights and interests of the victims'. The law was silent on the question of the responsibility of the parent company and the problem of enterprises that declare themselves bankrupt in order to avoid paying the fines levied.[14]

The working group on contemporary forms of slavery of the sub-commission has revitalized the concept of slavery by including in its definition trafficking, the exploitation of domestic migrant workers, and the misuse of the internet for the purposes of sexual exploitation.

The sub-commission decided to create its own global Social Forum. This is a two-day event on economic, social and cultural rights that will be organized annually, in recognition of the 'need for new process/mechanism within the UN system with broad participation, reflecting the current structure of international society'.[15] For the 2004 session on rural poverty, development and the rights of peasants and rural communities, invitations were extended to:

> Non-governmental organizations in consultative status with the Economic and Social Council and other non-governmental organizations outside Geneva, and in particular newly emerging actors, such as smaller groups and rural associations of the South, grass-roots organizations, peasant and farmers' organizations and their national and international associations, pastor-

alist associations, fishermen's/women's organizations, voluntary organizations, youth associations, community organizations, trade unions and associations of workers, representatives of the private sector, United Nations agencies, the relevant functional commissions of the Economic and Social Council, the regional economic commissions, international financial institutions and development agencies.

Whether the initiative will work remains to be seen. Perhaps funding the travel of all sub-commission members to Porte Allegre or wherever the World Social Forum meets, would have been a nice alternative.

UN High Commissioner for Human Rights The office of the High Commissioner for Human Rights has produced a set of papers on human rights and trade that go far beyond the only official WTO position on the issue, namely that the inclusion of core labour standards in WTO agreements should be resisted. The first Singapore WTO Ministerial Conference took the view in December 1996 that the International Labour Organization, and not the WTO, was the competent body to set and deal with these standards.

The High Commissioner's papers demonstrate that trade and human rights may be linked in many other ways, such as by monitoring the impact of trade rules on the rights of the vulnerable, marginalized and excluded; adopting a progressive approach to trade liberalization that allows taking into account the needs of those who could lose out as a result of the reform process; promoting corporate social responsibility etc. The High Commissioner's papers certainly do not take aim at the WTO as such. They are exercises in mainstreaming, i.e. in taking human rights to the building next door. The WTO and the human rights institutions occupy adjoining buildings beside the lake.

Geneva

Box 5.7 Office of the High Commissioner for Human Rights: Papers on Human Rights, Trade and Investment

- The Impact of the TRIPs Agreement on the Enjoyment of all Human Rights, Report of the High Commissioner for Human Rights, UN doc. E/CN.4/Sub.2/2001/13 (27 June 2001)
- Globalization and its Impact on the Full Enjoyment of Human Rights, Report of the High Commissioner for Human Rights, UN doc. E/CN.4/2002/54 (15 January 2002). The report considers the WTO's Agreement on Agriculture
- Liberalization of Trade in Services and Human Rights, Report of the High Commissioner for Human Rights, UN doc. E/CN.4/Sub.2/2002/9 (25 June 2002)
- Human Rights, Trade and Investment, Report of the High Commissioner for Human Rights, UN doc. E/CN.4/Sub.2/2003/9 (2 July 2003)

The Office of the High Commissioner also produced a submission to the fifth WTO Ministerial Conference (September 2003) on 'human rights and trade' that usefully summarizes and illustrates issues developed in the other papers. A fifth paper on human rights and the Millennium Development Goals is in preparation. All documents are available from the High Commissioner's website at <http://www.unhchr.ch>

Three initiatives of interest

The initiatives highlighted below all attempt to create or reinforce human rights obligations for economically dominant actors. The most comprehensive initiative is the effort to breathe life into the right to development, which aims at establishing a shared responsibility for human rights.

The right to development At a debate at Maastricht University some years ago, one colleague argued that the right to development was a Sleeping Beauty; the other that she was best left sleeping.[16] The UN Commission on Human Rights has both a working group (consisting of members of the Commission), and an individual expert on the right to development involved in waking her up, but she is not yet on her feet.

In the 1970s Karel Vasak (1972) launched a new category of human rights, called 'solidarity rights'. Solidarity rights sought to infuse the human dimension into areas where it had been missing, such as development. The holders of the right to development were not only individuals, but also states and sub-national groups. Duties were borne not only by the domestic state, but also by the international community as a whole. Only if all actors on the international social scene participated both as holders and duty bearers would the right to development be realized.

In 1986 the UN General Assembly adopted a non-binding UN Declaration on the Right to Development.[17] The declaration identified both individuals and peoples as holders, but offered little detail on the collective dimension of the right. The national state was primarily responsible for development. International responsibilities extended to no more than a cautiously worded duty to take steps to formulate international development policies. Vasak's idea was therefore taken up only partially.

The United States opposed the declaration, and a number of developed countries abstained. Nevertheless, the right to development also appears in subsequent texts that were adopted by consensus at the 1993 World Conference on Human Rights, and more recently at the Millennium General Assembly. The

Millennium Declaration[18] states: 'We are committed to making the right to development a reality for everyone and to freeing the entire race from want.' This is an incredible statement, given the strong opposition of most developed states to proposals that would equip the right to development with an implementation mechanism.

According to the Commission's individual expert, there are 'no countries currently implementing the right to development'![19] Arjun Sengupta (from India) is an economist who served as an executive director of the International Monetary Fund. The individual expert believes 'that it is possible to build upon a market-oriented approach to development, an approach based on liberalization and deregulation of economic policy to encourage private initiatives that not only promotes a high rate of economic growth with equity but realises social development goals as human rights'.[20] Sengupta promotes the idea of a right to a development *compact*:

> A mechanism for ensuring that all stakeholders recognize the 'mutuality of obligations', so that the obligations of developing countries to carry out rights-based programmes are matched by reciprocal obligations of the international community to cooperate to enable the implementation of the programmes. The purpose of development compacts is to assure the developing countries that if they fulfil their obligations, the programme for realizing the right to development will not be disrupted owing to lack of financing.[21]

The compact could focus on a few rights, such as those most closely related to the Millennium Development Goals. Developing countries should design a national programme in consultation with civil society aiming at the realization of these rights. The programme should be matched by obligations of the international community. A fund needs to be established with contributions in the form of 'callable commitments' from all the members of the Development Assistance Committee (DAC) of the Organisation for Economic Co-operation and Development (OECD). The compact is based on 'mutual responsibilities';[22] the obligations of the members of the international community are activated as soon as the relevant state recognizes and implements its national obligations.

The idea of matching needs of developing countries and offers of donors also appears in mainstream initiatives such as the poverty reduction strategy/comprehensive development framework approach or the New Partnership for Africa's Development (NEPAD) initiative. The compact differs from these initiatives in its focus on human rights and the concomitant emphasis on obligations of various actors. At a visit to the headquarters of the International Monetary Fund,[23] the individual expert encountered stiff resistance to the notion that the compact would impose (human rights) obligations on the IMF. The IMF would accept obligations to its members only under its constituent documents. Cries of loss of sovereignty were heard, not unlike those emanating from states when the international human rights system was first developed.

After numerous reports, little more can be added to the idea. What is missing is political support. The individual expert has been trying to get a donor-sponsored conference on the compact off the ground, but so far his efforts have been to no avail. The idea has not caught on in mainstream UN development fora.

The Commission's own working group does not fully agree either, but then the working group does not agree on anything. It even failed to agree its own report in 2003. Desperate for a way out of the deadlock, the Commission requested its sub-commission to take over. This is not as silly as it first sounds. The individual experts from developed countries in the sub-commission do not necessarily agree with the politics of their home governments.

Geneva

This has enabled the sub-commission to operate in a consensus mode, even when the Commission was deeply divided. The only difficulty is that at some point in the future the issue will boomerang back to the Commission. In the meantime, the working group can continue performing its rituals. In 2004, the Commission, at the request of the working group, decided to establish a high-level task force for one year, consisting of representatives from trade, finance and development institutions.[24]

Addressing the international financial institutions The Commission on Human Rights has an independent expert on the effects of structural adjustment policies and foreign debt and a working group elaborating 'basic policy guidelines on structural adjustment programs and economic, social and cultural rights'.[25]

At the international financial institutions, new policies were designed that, at least in principle, facilitate linking up to human rights. The HIPC (heavily indebted poor countries) initiative (in 1996) and the poverty reduction strategies (in 1999) are designed to make poverty reduction a more explicit element of the international financial institutions' policy (cf. Darrow 2003: 41–3). Countries seeking support for debt relief are required to prepare a comprehensive poverty reduction strategy paper (PRSP), with broad participation of civil society, key donors and the IFIs. The IFIs still support the macroeconomic policies they have always supported, but the declared intention now is to improve the alignment with social goals.

In July 2001, the chair of the Committee on ESC Rights wrote to the Office of the High Commissioner to suggest that the office should develop human rights guidelines for the new poverty reduction strategies. The aim was to ensure that countries negotiating with the international financial institutions took into account their human rights obligations. If human rights are not integrated into what is, in effect, a country's development plan on attacking poverty, they stand little chance of being prioritized. Countries can use a little support. References to human rights are absent from the IFI's joint staff guidelines for assessing the poverty reduction strategies.[26] The World Bank has initiated in-house training on human rights, including a two-day seminar held together with the Office of the High Commissioner.[27]

A team of three experts drew up the human rights guidelines. The draft was published in September 2002, and is available on the High Commissioner's website. The guidelines are to be piloted through substantive consultations and field-testing until the end of 2004, but by the time the guidelines were published, a significant group of countries had already submitted their poverty reduction strategies. On the other hand, the PRSP process is an ongoing one, and adjustments are possible during implementation.

Some Special Rapporteurs also engage with the international financial institutions. The newly established Special Rapporteur on the right to health, Paul Hunt (from New Zealand), immediately held informal discussions with IFI staff in Washington and intends to examine a selection of poverty reduction strategies through the prism of the right to health.[28] The dialogue of the former Special Rapporteur on the right to education, Katarina Tomasevski (from Denmark/Croatia), with the World Bank, she tells us, took 'a great deal of patience'.[29] The main bone of contention was the World Bank's position regarding school fees. Her reports contain numerous references to a division of opinion within the Bank on whether shifting the cost of education away from the state to individuals, families and communities is an acceptable strategy. The Special Rapporteur convincingly argues that human rights require a priority for education in fiscal allocations, and that a rights approach inevitably implies that education is not a service that can be traded commercially, but

115

an individual entitlement. Her recommendation to the Bank is to assess the conformity of its policy and practice in education lending with the international human rights obligations of its borrowers.[30]

In the summer of 1999, Tomasevski visited Uganda, the first highly indebted poor country to receive debt relief under the HIPC initiative. She discovered there was a real conflict between Uganda's debt repayment and human rights obligations with regard to resource allocation: 'The two types of obligation pull in opposite directions – debt repayment towards diminishing governmental allocations for education and human rights obligations towards increasing such allocations.'[31] During her visit, she found 'a great imbalance' between the high priority attached to debt servicing among the international and domestic actors she talked to and the paucity of attention paid to Uganda's international human rights obligations, including uncertainty as to what these obligations were and what they entailed in the area of education, and the poor translation of international obligations into domestic human rights safeguards.

The UN Committee on ESC Rights noted that some of the structural obstacles confronting developing states' anti-poverty strategies 'lie beyond their control in the contemporary international order'. Unless these obstacles, which include unsustainable foreign debt, are removed, 'the national anti-poverty strategies of some states have limited chance of sustainable success'.[32]

The demands made by the international financial institutions in the pursuit of macroeconomic policy should not limit the 'available resources' required to meet human rights obligations. Countries genuinely committed to human rights can use them as a shield 'to protect their poor from international policies that would otherwise cause avoidable hardship to vulnerable individuals and groups' (Hunt 2003: 146).

Norms on the responsibilities of transnational corporations and other business enterprises In August 2003, the sub-commission on the promotion and protection of human rights adopted by consensus[33] Norms on the responsibilities of transnational corporations and other business enterprises with regard to human rights,[34] together with a commentary[35] that is intended to provide practical interpretation. The working group which prepared the document will continue for at least another year to ensure follow-up on the adoption of the text.

Approval by the sub-commission is not the end of the drafting process. The text is now with the Commission 'for consideration and adoption'. Consensus at the Commission was not forthcoming. The Commission played for time, and requested the High Commissioner to produce a further report. Given the political divisions on the issue, it is unlikely that any redraft by the Commission would constitute an improvement over the current text. Perhaps no body higher up in the UN hierarchy than the sub-commission will ever adopt the Norms. This may not matter too much. Everything depends on the support the Norms will gather among states, international organizations, the business community and non-governmental organizations. Amnesty International, for instance, quickly decided to publish a brochure on the Norms aiming to strengthen their legal basis and calling on governments, companies and advocates to disseminate and apply the Norms (Amnesty International 2004: 4).

The Norms are not the first text on corporate responsibility for human rights. In 1977, the International Labour Organization adopted a Tripartite Declaration of Principles on Multinationals and Social Policy,[36] the scope of which, except for one general reference to the Universal Declaration on Human Rights, is limited to labour rights. The OECD (Organization for Economic Cooperation and Development) issued guidelines on Multinational Enterprises in 1976. At the occasion of the revision

117

of the Guidelines in 2000, a general human rights clause was added, encouraging enterprises to 'respect the human rights of those affected by their activities consistent with the host government's international obligations and commitments'.[37] The OECD guidelines contain specific clauses on labour rights only. In 1999 the United Nations launched the Global Compact, through which the organization hopes to share its values and principles with the business community. This is a short text containing nine principles on human rights, labour and the environment, to which corporations can voluntarily subscribe. The Global Compact has developed into a forum for dialogue between the United Nations, the corporate world and the NGO community.[38] All these documents are non-binding; none has a strong follow-up mechanism. In comparison, the scope of the sub-commission's Norms is more comprehensive, in that it covers the whole range of rights relevant to corporate activity.

The sub-commission discussed at length whether or not the Norms were binding. According to the main proponent of the text, expert David Weissbrodt, they were because they applied 'human rights law under ratified conventions to the activities of transnational corporations and other business enterprises'.[39] The Norms simply clarified existing law. Their content was not new. Bits and pieces from different binding treaties were brought together, and their application to companies clarified. It followed that adherence to the Norms was 'not entirely voluntary',[40] as companies were already bound (perhaps unwittingly!) by these obligations under international human rights law.

The Weissbrodt approach adds a nice twist, as the sub-commission is clearly incapable of adopting texts that bind and coerce states without their consent, let alone companies. Senior sub-commission expert Asbjorn Eide added, sphinx-like, that 'the future would clarify the status of the Norms as binding or otherwise'.[41] Lawyers grumble in the background, but a deferral of the matter to the course of time makes some sense; the sub-commission simply cannot do more. Ambivalence does not necessarily reduce the potential of the Norms. Non-binding Norms are not necessarily complied with less than binding ones. Other factors, such as the political context in which the rules are adopted, the precision of the rules, the cost of non-compliance and, above all, the credibility of the (future) implementation mechanism may be at least as important (Shelton 2000: 13–17).

The Norms apply both to domestic and transnational enterprises, but focus on the latter. Domestic companies were included in order to avoid loopholes by which transnational companies could escape application, and to ensure that subcontractors (such as sweatshops producing textiles for international brands) are also covered. Consequently, the Norms somewhat awkwardly state that they apply 'as a matter of practice' if the local business has a relationship with a transnational corporation or when the impact of its activities is not entirely local. The Norms always apply, however, when the local enterprise violates security rights.

The first operational paragraph (Boc 5.8) introduces the notion that states and companies share responsibility for human rights. The recognition of a corporate human rights responsibility does not diminish the responsibility of states. States remain primarily responsible, also, when companies commit abuses. If states do not offer protection against such abuses – in law and in practice – *they* violate human rights. In addition, the Norms establish an autonomous, direct corporate responsibility for human rights, limited to the company's 'sphere of activity and influence'. The novelty of the Norms resides in the fact that they attempt to describe this direct corporate responsibility for human rights as comprehensively as possible. Corporate human rights responsibility extends to the right to equal opportunity and non-discriminatory treatment, the right to security of persons, the

> **Box 5.8 UN Sub-Commission on the Promotion and Protection of Human Rights: Norms on the Responsibilities of Transnational Corporations and Other Business Enterprises (13 August 2003), par. 1**
>
> States have the primary responsibility to promote, secure the fulfilment of, respect, ensure respect of and protect human rights recognized in international as well as national law, including ensuring that transnational corporations and other business enterprises respect human rights. Within their respective spheres of activity and influence, transnational corporations and other business enterprises have the obligation to promote, secure the fulfilment of, respect, ensure respect of and protect human rights recognized in international as well as national law, including the rights and interests of indigenous peoples and other vulnerable groups.

rights of workers, the respect for national sovereignty and human rights, obligations with regard to consumer protection, and to obligations with regard to environmental protection.

The final section of the Norms deals with implementation mechanisms. This section needs to be understood as a compilation of suggestions on how implementation of the Norms could be ensured. Many of the suggested mechanisms do not yet exist. The sub-commission does not have the power to create them, nor does the body have the power to force others to create them.

The Norms 'require' that each company adopts internal rules of operation that reflect the content of the Norms, and incorporates the text in all its contractual arrangements. Companies are to be subjected to periodic monitoring and verification by United Nations, other international and national mechanisms already in existence or yet to be created, regarding their application of the Norms. In addition, companies are to provide prompt, effective and adequate reparation to persons, entities and communities that have been adversely affected by failure to comply with the Norms. In connection with determining damages in regard to criminal sanctions, and in all other respects, the Norms are to be applied by national courts and/or international tribunals, pursuant to national and international law.

Does Geneva matter?

The contribution of the Geneva system to the subject of globalization and human rights can be assessed in different ways. Over the years, the system has developed a number of functions, procedures and so on. Some of these now tackle globalization. Progress can still be made on how the institutions deal with the issue. Much of the literature on the Geneva system adopts this type of perspective. A harsher test, however, looks at the impact of the system on major actors in international economic relations, or at whether the system offers any hope of improvement of living conditions to those adversely affected by globalization.

The insider's view Rodley identifies three major functions fulfilled by both the charter-based and treaty bodies. He distinguishes between 'general country work', 'case specific work' and 'general overview activity' (Rodley 2003: 890).

In the general country work, there is a degree of interest in the impact of globalization, as evidenced by the work of the UN Committee on Economic, Social and Cultural Rights and by some of the thematic rapporteurs. Although Special Rapporteurs take their mandate from the Commission and the sub-commission, they enjoy a huge amount of discretion in fulfilling their task. To what extent they give attention to the impact of globalization depends on how they judge that impact personally. The UN Committee on ESC Rights takes a more systematic approach, but its expertise is limited, and its observations on the impact of globalization in the context of the reporting procedure tend to be fairly general, if not repetitive.

Non-governmental organizations can offer the perspective of those adversely affected by globalization both by supplying information to the treaty bodies during the reporting procedure and by accessing Special Rapporteurs directly. Missions are essential because of their local visibility and because they allow contacts with NGOs that may not be able to travel to Geneva. Ultimately, missions remain dependent on the consent of the relevant country.

Although case work is an important overall function of the Geneva human rights system, it is absent in the area of globalization and human rights. The problem is not that there are no cases; the problem is that the Geneva system does not provide a channel for dealing with them. An individual complaints procedure on economic, social and cultural rights could serve as a port of entry.

That leaves the 'general overview' activity. In our field of study, the category relates to work on the conceptual relationship between globalization and human rights; the clarification of the obligations and impact of non-state actors, and to efforts at human rights standard-setting specifically addressing the current international economic context. These functions are not unlike the role fulfilled by a policy-orientated research centre. In principle, the Geneva system enjoys the comparative advantage of being close to decision-makers; in principle, because there is no guarantee that research findings are taken up, particularly in areas that are politically contentious. Worse, the degree of disconnection between reports and resolutions in the area of globalization and human rights is astounding. Resolutions reflect political debates between governments, but frequently fail to provide a response to expert studies. One can take a hopeful view, and argue that the reports are in fact more important than the resolutions, because they lead their own life. They are definitely noticed more than an academic piece in a human rights journal, and do contribute to making the issues discussed visible at the international level (cf. Gomez 2003: 79).

If Geneva does perform the role of a policy-orientated research centre on globalization and human rights, it may well suffer from lack of staff. The more outspoken Special Rapporteurs complain about lack of support from the Office of the High Commissioner. In October 2003, the Special Rapporteur on the right to education launched a formal complaint against the Office of the High Commissioner, lamenting lack of support for 'her efforts to enhance the visibility of the right to education' and questioning the delay in the processing of her mission report (on China). The increase in obstacles and difficulties in the carrying out of her mandate resulted in her recommendation to the Commission in 2004 not to renew her mandate.[42] The independent expert on structural adjustment complained of an 'inflexible interpretation and application of the rules regarding disbursement of resources coupled with a lack of enthusiasm on the part of Governments to provide additional resources'.[43] The senior member of the sub-commission from Cuba, Miguel Alfonso Martinez, produced a report on 'human rights and human responsibilities'[44] full of outrage about questionnaires gone missing and translations delayed, only to find a prolongation of his project rejected by the Commission by a vote of 25 to 25.[45]

The Special Rapporteur on the right to housing offers sobering comments on the ability of the Geneva human rights system to influence major UN events related to globalization. The Special Rapporteur attended or contributed to a number of global conferences, such as the World Summit on Sustainable Development, the Habitat Istanbul +5 Conference, the third UNCTAD Conference on Least Developed Countries and others. He notes: 'In

123

contributing to these global conferences, the Special Rapporteur was particularly concerned at the lack of references to relevant human rights instruments and to the work of treaty bodies and the United Nations human rights mechanisms in draft outcome documents and background papers.'[46]

On some occasions the final documents included references to human rights, but not always. Clearly, it is not because Geneva takes up an issue from a human rights perspective that the whole UN system follows suit. One exception is the International Labour Organization, the specialized agency that has traditionally adopted a rights approach. The ILO took a major parallel initiative on the social dimension of globalization, which included the establishment in February 2002 of a World Commission on the Social Dimension of Globalization, presided over by the Tanzanian and Finnish presidents. The final report of the World Commission[47] contains a large number of recommendations, including the setting up a global parliamentary group to develop an integrated oversight of the major international financial and economic organizations, and of a 'Globalization Policy Forum' to bring together international organizations and other key actors and participants in global debates on globalization and its social impact, and the design of global economic and social policies.

Taking up human rights struggles: the Landless Workers Movement of Brazil Does the Geneva system reflect the realities of local human rights struggles? Does the Geneva system offer a valid response to abuses suffered by those marginalized by state and market?

Following Baxi's approach, in an ideal world, peoples and communities are the primary authors of human rights. Their resistance to (abusive) power 'at a second order level, [is] translated into standards and norms adopted by a community of

Box 5.9 Our Father

In April 2001, I attended the inauguration of a monument in honour of Antonio Tavares Pereira, a farmer who was killed when the police stopped an MST-organized demonstration. The monument was erected in a field next to a motorway leading into the town of Curitiba. The ceremony lasted for three hours, and included speeches, chanting and poetry. There were also common prayers, like 'Our Father who is in heaven' that were read out together by thousands of people. The version of the prayer used during the ceremony (credited to Antônio Pureza) differed from the original, however, and offers a perfect example of the ideological mix the MST subscribes to:

Our Father who is in heaven, a lot of people suffer from
   hunger.
But this is not your fault, hallowed be your name.
Oh, Our Father, your people suffer from hunger.
Your Kingdom of justice and equality come.
For this earth to be of all, your will be done.
Oh, Our Father, someone is in need.
Give us this day our daily bread, each day as you will,
Forgive us our trespasses if I forgive truly.
Oh, Our Father, forgive us our sins.
Deliver us from the temptation of one modern country,
That already lived independence and today is indebted.
Oh, Our Father, someone was guilty.
Deliver us from the evils of globalization and of the IMF,
   which are ruining the nation.
Oh, Our Father, listen to this lamentation.
Oh, oh, Our Father, I beg pardon,
Oh, oh, forgive our brothers ...

states. In the making of human rights it is the local that translates into global languages the reality of their aspiration for a just world' (Baxi 2002: 101).

In today's world, the role of 'translating the local into global languages' falls to the Geneva human rights system. The Geneva system represents the international community's efforts to establish a global human rights institution. Not by a long way is that system geared towards 'the primary authors of human rights'. It is, like much of the international order, intergovernmental in nature, even if access mechanisms allowing civil society participation have been created. The argument for maintaining the intergovernmental nature of the system is that governments are the main duty bearers in human rights, and that no human rights duties can be created unless governments consent. Consequently, international negotiations on human rights making have led to debates among governments about what is acceptable to them. Governments may even decide to shut the doors on participation by others, as they did in the final stages of the 1993 World Conference on Human Rights. The primary objective is the achievement of consensus between states. There is a real risk that grassroots human rights experiences, as reflected in the practice of social movements, are lost in translation.

An example may help to clarify the point. The Landless Workers Movement (MST) in Brazil is one of the largest social movements in Latin America. The MST was created in 1984, and arose from a collaboration between Catholic priests adhering to liberation theology, left-wing political activists committed to variations of Maoism, Marxism or social democracy and the rural poor (cf. Wright and Wolford 2003). Added to this cocktail is a strong shot of Brazilian nationalism: reclaiming land is also reclaiming Brazil for its people. The unlikely alliance gathered to challenge the highly unequal distribution of land ownership in Brazil. MST took direct action and organized occupations of unproductive (i.e. fallow) land which, under the constitutionally declared objectives of land reform, was fit for expropriation by the state and distribution to the landless. The MST set up communities of settlers, including its own schools system. Its land occupation strategy relied on securing subsequent governmental recognition, formal expropriation and government funding to assist in production and basic amenities. The MST position in law is somewhat ambivalent (cf. Meszaros 2000). It claims that the land occupations are not illegal – even though they may well be technically – because the landless are implementing a constitutional provision on which successive governments have failed to deliver. In theory, at least, there is a revolutionary, albeit non-violent, strand in the MST's commitment to the expropriation of all large farms for the benefit of collective production. On the other hand, there is a large degree of cooperation with benevolent state institutions (Wright and Wolford 2003: 309).

Today, the MST is a hierarchically structured massive social movement, organized in twenty-three out of the twenty-seven Brazilian states, with an estimated 1.5 million members. Ideologically the movement remains very much to the left, although the support from sections of the Catholic Church remains intact. The MST has become increasingly involved in tackling the impact of economic globalization, particularly since the Brazilian government decided to adopt a World Bank-supported scheme on market-assisted land reform in 1999, involving the government buying land from landlords and selling it to individual farmers who were then required to secure credit to finance production. Government funds were shifted from the governmental agency responsible for expropriations to a newly established Land Bank. As a side effect, the scheme significantly reduced the potential for success of the MST land occupation strategy.

The MST is an important player on the domestic political scene. Relationships with left-wing parties, including with current President Lula da Silva's Workers' Party are good. An increasing number of MST members compete directly in elections. Unlike many other social movements, the MST does not need the international system to conquer domestic political space. The MST's approach to the international level has been 'eclectic and strategic' (cf. Rajagopal 2003: 252). The organization is a member of Via Campesina, an international movement of peasant organizations, and is a major force in the World Social Forum. Occasional use is made of intergovernmental mechanisms to further the organization's goals. In 1999, the MST, together with other organizations representing landless farmers, twice challenged the implementation of the market-assisted land reform policy at the World Bank Inspection Panel, albeit unsuccessfully.[48]

The MST's relatively strong position in domestic politics does not protect its militants from political violence. Divisions in Brazilian society remain. The big landowners are still a major political force, and often exercise their own brand of law and order, particularly in the rural areas where the occupations take place. The MST has challenged the use of violence by police and paramilitary forces against landless farmers in the context of its land occupations, against MST demonstrations in the cities, and against leaders of the organization or of other peasant movements. Cases of rural violence, including killings, are rarely prosecuted, but if they are, they rarely end in convictions. The case of the Eldorado dos Carajás massacre did go to trial in 2002 in the state of Para, but the MST withdrew, arguing that the judges were subject to pressure from local politicians and landowners. The case involved the killing of nineteen landless peasants in 1996, during a protest roadblock organized by MST. The decision in the case – a limited number of police officers were convicted, but not arrested – is under appeal. The MST has equally taken the case to the Inter-American Commission of Human Rights, focusing particularly on the inadequacy of investigations by the military police.

The Commission on Human Rights' Special Rapporteur on extrajudicial, summary or arbitrary executions, Asma Jahangir (from Pakistan) visited Brazil in September 2003 for three weeks to investigate killings by paramilitary groups and police collusion. Two witnesses who gave testimony to her were killed while she was still on mission in the country, raising serious concerns about the government's and the United Nations' ability to provide protection to those willing to come forward. The Special Rapporteur was 'overwhelmed' with information about human rights violations perpetrated by the security forces, in particular the military police. She found that many of the reports were backed by evidence which strongly indicated that these grave abuses were committed with impunity.[49]

In rural areas, the cause of extrajudicial killings is often the struggle over land. Violations of civil and political rights are closely connected to the land reform issue. Uneven land distribution also has an impact on the whole range of economic, social and cultural rights. So does economic globalization, both in terms of the World Bank's involvement in market-assisted agrarian reform, as in the pressure to prioritize agricultural production for export. Strong, globally connected social movements, of which the MST is only one example, exist that enjoy sufficient domestic political space to relate to the experience of landless peasants. They are typically the group which tends to be marginalized by both state and market, and whose experience should therefore guide the global response. In addition, Brazil is not a forgotten country, nor is it a state that isolates itself from the international community. At first sight, the conditions for the translation of a local experience into a global approach appear to be fulfilled.

In 2003, the UN Committee on Economic, Social and Cultural Rights adopted 'concluding observations'[50] about Brazil's initial report to the committee.[51] This initial report should have been delivered in 1994, but was not in fact ready until 2001. The government was pushed by a coalition of sixty Brazilian NGOs that had *previously* produced a 150-page alternative report, which it had presented over an informal lunch attended by nearly all members of the committee. In its concluding observations, the committee lists the participation of civil society in the monitoring of the Covenant as a positive factor and encourages the government to continue to consult with civil society when preparing its next report.

The committee urges the government to take legal action against those responsible for committing crimes against landless farmers. Special attention is given to the situation of indigenous peoples. The government should take into account the Covenant when it negotiates with the international financial institutions. On the crucial issue of land reform, the Committee:

> 31. Notes with concern the high concentration of land in the hands of a minority, and its negative effects on the equitable distribution of wealth.
>
> 61. Urges the state party to undertake appropriate measures to ensure effective realization of agrarian reform.

The observations are disappointing because they give no direction. Any reform policy satisfies the recommendations, and so even their potential impact on Brazil or at the international level is limited. The observations do not even provide civil society with an instrument for leverage.

The Special Rapporteur on the right to food, Jean Ziegler (from Switzerland), went on mission to Brazil from 1 to 18 March 2002,[52] before the current government came to office. The Special Rapporteur expresses his appreciation of the 'very vital' NGOs and social movements that met with him. He quotes an MST leader who expresses the opinion that Brazil's market model creates poverty. According to the Special Rapporteur, the role of the MST in agrarian reform is 'overall a beneficial one'. He approves of the activities of communities set up in occupied land.

He finds that growth in agricultural production has not eradicated hunger. The market model has proved insufficient to guarantee the right to food: 'export orientation of agriculture and the import of cheaper food crops has also failed to feed all the poor'. The current economic model 'should be reviewed to examine the impacts of macroeconomic policy and trade liberalization on poverty and social inequality'. Agrarian reform should be speeded up. Resistance in some quarters of the political and economic elite to agrarian reform 'should be challenged, by offering compensation for land but without resorting to market-based mechanisms of land reform if these do not provide effective redistribution'.

The Commission on Human Rights heard the Special Rapporteur at its 2003 session, as it does every year. The resolution on the right to food[53] adopted at the end of the session *does not refer at all* to the Special Rapporteur's mission to Brazil. None of his recommendations is taken up. The Commission did decide to extend the Special Rapporteur's mandate for a further three years, to the sole and forlorn opposition of the United States.

It is intolerable, the resolution declares with some passion, that 'there are around 840 million undernourished people in the world and that every seven seconds a child under the age of 10 dies, directly or indirectly of hunger somewhere in the world'.

Some of these people are in Brazil.

Notes

1 UN Commission on Human Rights, Resolution 2003/18 (22 April 2003), par. 13.

2 Examples include the concluding observations on Slovakia, Poland and Georgia, UN Committee on ESC Rights, UN doc. E/C.12/1/Add. 81, 82, 83 (19 December 2002), and on Moldova, UN Committee on ESC rights, UN doc. E/C.12/1/Add. 91 (12 December 2003).

3 Concluding observations on Brazil, UN Committee on ESC Rights, UN doc. E/C.12/1/Add. 87 (26 June 2003).

4 Concluding observations on Ireland, UN Committee on ESC Rights, UN doc. E/C.12/1/Add. 77 (5 June 2002).

5 Concluding observations on Brazil, UN Committee on ESC Rights, UN doc. E/C.12/1/Add. 87 (26 June 2003).

6 UN Committee on ESC Rights, 'Statement on Poverty and the International Covenant on Economic, Social and Cultural Rights', UN doc. E/C.12/2001/10 (10 May 2001).

7 UN Committee on ESC Rights, 'General Comment no. 15: The Right to Water', UN doc. E/C.12/2002/11 (20 January 2003).

8 Ibid., par. 24.

9 Similar recommendations appear in the recent UN Committee on the Rights of the Child, 'General Comment no. 5: General Measures of Implementation for the Convention on the Rights of the Child', UN doc. CRC/GC/2003/5 (3 October 2003), pars 42–4.

10 UN doc. E/CN.4/Sub.2/2003/14 (25 June 2003).

11 UN Commission on Human Rights, Resolution 2003/23 (22 April 2003), adopted by 38 to 15 votes.

12 UN doc. E/CN.4/2003/5/Add. 2 (3 February 2003).

13 Ibid., par. 49.

14 UN doc. E/CN.4/2004/46/Add. 2 (19 December 2003), par. 105.

15 UN Sub-Commission on the Protection and the Promotion of Human Rights, Resolution 2003/14 (13 August 2003).

16 Nico Schrijver and Gudmundur Alfredsson.

17 UN General Assembly Resolution 41/128 (4 December 1986), adopted by 146 to 1 votes with 8 abstentions.

18 UN General Assembly Resolution 55/2 (8 September 2000).

19 UN doc. E/CN.4/2003/26 (24 March 2003), par. 26.

20 UN doc. E/CN.4/2002/WG.18/6 (18 September 2002), par. 19.

21 Ibid., par. 14.

22 UN doc. E/CN.4/2003/26 (24 March 2003), par. 25.

23 UN doc. E/CN.4/2002/WG.18/2/Add. 1 (5 March 2002), pars 16–25.

24 UN Commission on Human Rights, Resolution 2004/7 (13 April 2004), adopted by 49 to 3 votes.

25 E.g. see UN Commission on Human Rights, Resolution 2002/29 (22 April 2002).

26 The Joint Staff Assessment Guidelines appear in Annex 2 to

IMF/IDA, *Poverty Reduction Strategy Papers. Progress in Implementation* (Washington: IMF/IDA, 2001).

27 UN doc. E/CN.4/Sub.2/2003/14 (25 June 2003), par. 30.

28 UN doc. E/CN.4/2003/58 (13 February 2003). For a first attempt with respect to Niger's poverty reduction strategy, see UN doc. E/CN.4/2004 (16 February 2004), pars 57–75.

29 UN doc. E/CN.4/2001/52 (11 January 2001), par. 32.

30 UN doc. E/CN.4/2003/9 (21 January 2003), par. 9.

31 UN doc. E/CN.4/2000/6/Add. 1 (9 August 1999), par. 35.

32 UN doc. E/C.12/2001/10 (10 May 2001).

33 UN Sub-Commission Resolution 2003/16 (13 August 2003), adopted without a vote.

34 UN doc. E/CN.4/Sub.2/2003/12/Rev.2 (26 August 2003).

35 UN doc. E/CN.4/Sub.2/2003/38/Rev.2 (26 August 2003).

36 ILO Tripartite Declaration of Principles on Multinationals and Social Policy (16 November 1977), available from the ILO website <www.ilo.org>

37 Article II, 2, OECD Guidelines on Multinational Enterprises (27 June 2000), available from the OECD website on <www.oecd.org> or in printed form as OECD doc. DAFFE/IME/WPG (2000) 15/final (31 October 2001).

38 The Global Compact (31 January 1999) is available from the Global Compact website <www.unglobalcompact.org>

39 UN doc. E/CN.4/Sub.2:2002/13 (15 August 2002), par. 14.

40 UN doc. E/CN.4/Sub.2/2003/13 (6 August 2003), par. 12.

41 Ibid., par. 14.

42 UN doc. E/CN.4/2004/45 (15 January 2004).

43 Bernards Mudho in UN doc. E/CN.4/2003/10 (23 October 2002), par. 70.

44. UN doc. E/CN.4/2003/15 (17 March 2003).

45 See UN doc. E/CN/4/2003/135 (no date), par. 527. The vote was on an amendment proposing the prolongation.

46 UN doc. E/CN.4/2003/5 (3 March 2003), par. 8.

47 World Commission on the Social Dimension of Globalization (2004), 'A Fair Globalization: Creating Opportunities for All' (Geneva: ILO, 2004). For the full report and background information, see <www.ilo.org/public/english/wcsdg>

48 World Bank Inspection Panel, Report and Recommendation on Second Request for Inspection on Brazil: Land Reform and Poverty

Alleviation Pilot Project (17 December 1999); and Report and Recommendation on Request for Inspection on Brazil: Land Reform and Poverty Alleviation Pilot Project (27 May 1999).

49 UN doc. E/CN.4/2004/7/Add. 3 (28 January 2004).

50 UN doc. E/CN.12/1/Add. 87 (26 June 2003).

51 UN doc. E/1990/5/Add. 53 (20 November 2001).

52 See UN doc. E/CN.4/2003/54/Add. 1 (3 January 2003).

53 UN Commission on Human Rights, Resolution 2003/25 (22 April 2003), adopted by 51 to 1 (United States) votes, with one abstention (Australia).

6 | Avenues of hope

The experiences of social movements and non-governmental organizations that have relied on human rights to achieve their objectives inform the structure of this chapter. In different places, the Social and Economic Rights Action Centre (SERAC) in Nigeria serves as a guide, because it has used a huge variety of human rights instruments in the context of different campaigns. But so have other organizations, and some of their experiences are highlighted as well, particularly when the results are of interest to the further normative development of human rights. The chapter jumps from one institution to another, but this approach reflects the reality of how organizations of, or acting on behalf of, marginalized communities work with human rights.

Grassroots 'best practices' in achieving recognition of human rights violations require an ability to identify the optimal forum, i.e. the forum where the probability of recognition of the violation is the highest. Some human-rights-related institutions may have higher thresholds of entry than others, but the optimal choice depends primarily on the identity of the human rights duty holder. Options vary according to the perpetrator targeted. Different institutions deal with state responsibility, corporate responsibility, the international financial institutions, armed opposition groups and so on. The international human rights regime is fragmented, and therefore NGOs need to make strategic choices on their point of entry. The chosen level could be a global institution, a regional one, a domestic or foreign court, or a local institution, or a local community-based dispute settlement mechanism. Forum shopping and switching is essential.

One lesson that can be learned from observing NGO experiences in operating the human rights regime is that there may not be a 'preferred' level for dealing with all instances of human rights violations. It does not make sense for an NGO defending marginalized communities to focus all its human rights efforts on the Geneva system, or at the domestic level only. This is a consequence not only of the fragmentation of the human rights regime, but also of the globalization of human rights problems. Depending on the issue, a combination of institutions will have to be used. A campaign on access to treatment for AIDS may require involving domestic courts, foreign courts, the WTO dispute settlement system and self-regulatory bodies on corporate responsibility. An analysis from below of the global human rights regime does not insist so much on the prioritization of one institutional level over the other, but on the need to ensure that the regime as a whole offers the necessary guarantees that human rights claims are properly dealt with.

If a social movement or an NGO comes to the conclusion that the human rights regime does not provide sufficient avenues for dealing with an issue of concern, there is always the option of creating an alternative legal order. Groups may feel that they need to reclaim sovereignty on behalf of the group or the people, if all official institutions fail to acknowledge their suffering. The chapter opens with a discussion of peoples' tribunals, which seek to demonstrate to official courts that an alternative approach based on the living experiences of communities that suffer abuse is possible. The following section briefly returns to the Movement of Landless Workers (MST), one of the many organizations that has adopted the strategy.

Peoples' tribunals

In May 2001, MST and many other civil society organizations convened an 'international tribunal on the crimes of the *latifundio* and on the official policies of human rights violations' in

Curitiba, the capital of the state of Paraná in the south of Brazil. The tribunal met in a university auditorium packed with cheering MST supporters, and was widely reported upon in the local press. A member of the Inter-American Commission of Human Rights chaired. The jury consisted of both Brazilian and foreign judges, academics and politicians including Argentine Nobel Peace Prize-winner Adolfo Pérez Esquivel. All were selected by the organizers. International networks, such as Global Exchange and FIAN (the Food First Information and Action Network), as well as partner organizations from the North (such as 11.11.11, the coalition of the Flemish North–South Movement), contributed to the event.

The tribunal was 'a response of society' to the increased use of violence by the police, the Public Security Office and armed militias against encampments of landless families and to the imprisonment of supporters of agrarian reform.

Interestingly, the cases presented to the tribunal dealt with violations of civil and political rights. The human rights section of the MST website equally focuses on civil and political rights. This is somewhat odd, given that the major issue facing the organization – agrarian reform – can easily be framed in terms of ESC rights. In the following chapter, it is argued that there is much added value in approaching agrarian reform from a human rights angle.

The explanation is that the MST makes only an instrumental use of human rights. Human rights are not *the* normative framework for all its work. The MST is not a human rights organization, and there are grounds for human-rights-based criticism of the functioning of the organization. It took the MST a long time to come to terms with the issue of gender discrimination. The issue surfaced within the organization when land occupations were successful, and land titles that had been gained were handed over to the farmers. Women seldom qualified (Deere 2003: 257–88).

The organizers justified the convening of the tribunal as follows:

> It is in this context – where the state has proved incapable of upholding the established constitutional guarantees to its citizens and where impunity has been the general rule (not one of the crimes against the workers has been seriously investigated nor have the perpetrators or instigators been punished) – that the organizers in defence of human rights are organizing an International Tribunal [...] As a way of reaffirming the fundamental values consolidated in the Universal Declaration of Human Rights and in the International Treaties ratified by the Brazilian state, the Tribunal aims to symbolically replicate the due legal process neglected by the state.

Care was taken to mimic a legal procedure. The alleged culprit, the government of Paraná, was invited, but declined to participate. The regional chapter of the bar refused to appoint a defence lawyer *in absentia*. The state governor did produce a memorandum that was read out during the proceedings. The memorandum recalled that the state government had been legitimately elected, and was obedient to the constitution and human rights. The international tribunal was an 'exception tribunal' (that is, not legally established), and as such a threat to democracy, and an interference with the judicial process – a crime under Brazilian law punishable with between one and four years' imprisonment. According to the government of Paraná, the mock tribunal was no more than a clearly politically motivated theatrical event.

In response, the tribunal's prosecutor (from Argentina) admitted that trials were theatrical, whether they were organized by the state or by the people. He also recognized that the trial was politically orientated: all those participating in the trial were committed to human rights, and that was a political position.

In his words, the tribunal was 'impartial, but not neutral' in the face of human rights violations. The organizations convening the tribunal, he argued, were exercising their constitutional right to express their opinion.

The organizers presented the members of the jury with a long list of questions prepared in advance. According to the original schedule, the jury was given 'fifteen to thirty minutes' to deliberate in private on a response. Some of the questions dealt with issues that had not come up during the evidence, such as the responsibility of the national government for its lack of action on agrarian reform. At the insistence of the (foreign) members of the jury, those questions were struck off the list. Deliberations went on for two hours, much to the dismay of the audience (their singing and clapping reached the deliberation room) and of the press office. Nevertheless, the organizers must have felt happy about the event, as they decided to organize another tribunal in 2003 in Belém in the state of Pará.

International peoples' tribunals have a long pedigree. In 1966, the Welsh philosopher and Nobel Literature Prize-winner Bertrand Russell created an international war crimes tribunal to determine whether the United States and other governments had committed violations of international law during the Vietnam War. Jean-Paul Sartre served as the executive president of the first session of the tribunal. In later years the Russell Tribunal rendered judgment on authoritarian regimes in Latin America in the 1970s, on *berufsverbot* for political dissidents in Germany, and on the fate of indigenous populations.

Today, peoples' tribunals have become a global phenomenon. The Asian Human Rights Charter, a 'peoples' charter' endorsed by numerous Asian non-governmental groups and individuals on the occasion of the fiftieth anniversary of the Universal Declaration of Human Rights, perceives of peoples' tribunals as part of the machinery of enforcement of human rights:

Civil society institutions can help to enforce rights through the organization of Peoples' tribunals, which can touch the conscience of the government and the public. The establishment of Peoples' tribunals emphasizes that the responsibility for the protection of rights is wide, and not a preserve of the state. They are not confined to legal rules in their adjudication and can consequently help to uncover the moral and spiritual foundations of human rights.[1]

Peoples' tribunals come in all shapes and sizes. Procedures differ, and issues range from the global to the local:

- In Colombia, but also in Canada, international opinion tribunals tackled Colombia's involvement in crimes against humanity, and related issues of impunity.
- In Berlin, an unofficial European tribunal issued a judgment on NATO's involvement in the Yugoslavia war, on the same day the prosecutor of the official International Criminal Tribunal for former Yugoslavia announced that she saw no grounds to open an inquiry into the issue.
- In Tokyo, a women's international war crimes tribunal met in December 2000 to discuss sexual enslavement by the Japanese army during the Second World War, an issue neglected by the original Tokyo war crimes tribunal.
- In the United States and in India, trade unions regularly organize tribunals on workers' rights *and* corporate accountability.
- The Asian Human Rights Commission and a Thai human rights NGO organized an international peoples' tribunal on food scarcity and militarization in Burma from 1996 to 2000. This tribunal did not hear any evidence in public, for fear of reprisals against those testifying. The findings were presented at the UN Commission on Human Rights in Geneva. As a follow-up, the Asian Legal Resource Centre in 2003 established

a *permanent* peoples' tribunal on the right to food and the rule of law in Asia. The panel members are leading human rights advocates from India, Korea and Thailand.

A long-standing initiative is the Permanent Peoples' Tribunal created in 1979 by Lelio Basso, an Italian parliamentarian and a member of the original Russell Tribunal. The tribunal (now based in Rome) examines claims of violations of peoples' rights. Individual human rights violations are taken up only to the extent that they are connected to collective claims. The tribunal applies international law (including the Universal Declaration of Human Rights), but also non-state law such as the Algiers Declaration on the Rights of Peoples.[2] The tribunal also engages in standard-setting work. One example is the Charter on Industrial Hazards and Human Rights (1996), which it adopted in the wake of its judgment on the Bhopal case. The introduction to the charter clarifies that the text was not determined by diplomatic compromise, but 'rather, its substance, and hence its authority, derive directly from the collective experience of those who have been forced to live with the consequences of industrial hazards'.

The alternative charters and tribunals testify to the ambition of civil society organizations to assert normative prerogatives of their own. The organizations assert this prerogative because they wish to establish the truth about existing violations, and feel that official law and/or mechanisms, both international and domestic, offer no appropriate recourse. The existing legal order offers no adequate remedies. By default, a private initiative assumes what should otherwise be public functions, such as legislating or passing judgment. The private institution does so symbolically, without claming powers of enforcement, which remain the monopoly of the state.

Clearly, the tribunals have a political objective. Often the aim is the promotion of human rights or, more broadly, the

141

discovery of forms of human suffering that would otherwise remain hidden. The mock trials are campaigning techniques. Nevertheless, the choice of the legal discourse requires a degree of discipline. If basic principles of procedural fairness and due process are not respected, the tribunals defeat their own purpose. Regardless of whether use is made of state or non-state law, the reasoning should be legal and sound. Not every peoples' tribunal performs brilliantly in this respect.

This is not to suggest that only lawyers should sit on the tribunals. One of the writers who participated in the tribunals, Julio Cortázar, addressed the position of the non-lawyers. His concern was with the peoples in Latin America who were under authoritarian rule at the time, and who would face 'a wall of silence' on any activities the tribunal might adopt. This should not preoccupy the lawyers too much, Cortázar argued. Their job was to develop and apply the law as best as they could. It was the task of the non-lawyers on the tribunal, of a 'simple inventor of fiction' like himself, to ensure that awareness was raised about the tribunal's activities through any means that could touch the public: beauty, poetry, humour, irony, satire, caricature, images, sound, jokes, drama, drawings, gestures (Cortázar 1983: 9–10).

When peoples' tribunals are organized with the required rigour, they deserve attention, because they represent attempts at developing a human rights response to the needs of disenfranchised communities. The idea of reclaiming sovereignty in the face of repression has lost none of its strength.

The limitations of the initiatives are obvious. The judgments have no legal value whatsoever. Certainly, the tribunals are not an alternative to lobbying for reform of the current human rights regime, or to making the best possible use of the opportunities that the current regime can offer. The Social and Economic Rights Action Centre in Nigeria offers an interesting example of an organization that has firmly invested in the latter strategy.

Introducing the Social and Economic Rights Action Centre, Nigeria

The Social and Economic Rights Action Centre (SERAC) describes itself as:

> A non-governmental, non-partisan and voluntary initiative concerned with the promotion and protection of social and economic rights in Nigeria [...] SERAC seeks to build awareness about social and economic rights and explore strategies for securing their realization. In addition, SERAC aims at broadening access of individuals and communities, and strengthening their participation in the design and implementation of social and economic policies and programs, which affect them.

The organization was founded in May 1995, at a time when Nigeria was under the military rule of General Abacha, one of the worst periods of Nigeria's unenviable political history.

The MST and SERAC have little in common. Classification of civil society organizations is not straightforward, but the MST and SERAC certainly belong to different categories. The MST qualifies as a social movement, i.e. as 'an organized type of collective action that attempts to change the configuration of power within society, on the basis of a shared belief or identity' (cf. Gomez 2003: 60–5). SERAC, on the other hand, is a small urban-based non-membership NGO – a characteristic it shares with most human rights NGOs in Nigeria (Ibhawoh 2001: 86–97) – that offers its expertise to local social movements in the limited arena of human rights. In addition, the MST is formed by those who are directly threatened, while SERAC is assisting others whose rights are violated (cf. Hajib 2000). The MST has managed to avoid dependence on external assistance (Wright and Wolford 2003: 331). SERAC relies heavily on donors, in particular from North America and Europe. In 2000, SERAC acknowledged the support of, among others, the embassies to Nigeria of the Netherlands and Norway, the Ford Foundation and the World Council for Christian Communication.

It does not follow that SERAC is an elite organization far removed from social realities. It grew out of an initiative to support slum dwellers who were picked up by the police. Sometimes human-rights-based litigation achieved their liberation from prison, but their socioeconomic situation remained as before, and often the same people were picked up again later. In the analysis of SERAC's director, it was hard to mobilize against civil and political rights violations of the military regime, without addressing the daily problems of poor people: education, health, housing and employment (Hajib 2000).

SERAC currently combines legal action with community action. One example is its work with the Maroko community, a Lagos squatter community of 300,000 people that was removed from its original location in July 1990 on seven days' notice. SERAC assists the displaced community with legal action challenging the quality of the housing provided as resettlement and the denial of primary education to children of the demolished Maroko schools. The organization also set up an information centre for the community at the resettlement site in 1999, and it operates a microcredit project in the community targeting women and including human rights training.

SERAC's work is of particular interest because the organization works on local issues that connect to global problems, and because it identifies these problems in terms of domestic, regional and global norms. The organization links up well with various international NGOs, and thus channels information on the experiences of local communities to the global level. SERAC runs an international advocacy programme aimed at enhancing the organization's outreach, involving the dissemination of information on Nigeria's human rights practices.

In Nigeria, the African Charter on Human and Peoples' Rights is a key source of legal obligation in the field of economic and social rights. The African Charter is the only international human rights treaty incorporated into domestic law. Treaties that are not incorporated are not locally enforceable under the Nigerian constitution.

The constitution itself deals with economic, social and cultural rights in the chapter on fundamental objectives and directive principles of state policy. Nigerian courts have so far denied individuals the right to rely directly on these constitutional provisions in a court of law (cf. Abdullah 2000: 15). Consequently, the African Charter offers the only real legal avenue for enforcing economic and social rights. SERAC's reliance on the African Charter therefore does not necessarily reflect a principled stance in favour of regional human rights.

Two local issues of global interest on which SERAC has worked are the treatment of people living with AIDS and the demolition of homes in marginalized communities.

SERAC took up the first HIV discrimination lawsuit in Nigeria in February 2001. The case involved a nurse working in a hospital in a suburb of Lagos who was fired by the hospital's medical director on account of her HIV-positive status. SERAC argued that the termination of her employment on these grounds constituted a violation of the African Charter and Nigerian laws. The presiding judge denied the plaintiff access to the courtroom on the grounds that the judge herself and others in the courtroom might contract the virus as a result of the plaintiff's presence. At a later stage, the judge struck out the entire lawsuit, citing undue publicity as the reason. The case, now under appeal, attracted global attention. The plight of people affected by HIV/AIDS has brought together social movements, humanitarian and development organizations, human rights organizations and a number of governments both locally and globally (Nelson and Dorsey 2003: 2021–2).

SERAC also challenged house demolitions in the Lagos area. The organization cooperates with the Centre for Housing Rights and Eviction (COHRE), a Geneva-based human rights NGO working internationally. In October 2003 the Lagos state government commenced the eviction of an estimated 17,000 people from the Ijora-Badia community, giving residents less than twenty-four hours to vacate their homes. The forced eviction took place three days later, before the courts heard a legal challenge by SERAC of an earlier eviction of part of the same community. Interestingly, Amnesty International (AI) issued a press release on 31 October 2003 calling for a termination of the mass forced evictions, and qualifying them as a violation of the right to adequate housing. The press release was one of the first applications of AI's 2001 decision to extend its mandate to aspects of ESC rights. The AI press release twice refers to SERAC as a source backing up the Amnesty position.

In addition to seeking international alliances on domestic cases, SERAC has directly appealed to international mechanisms to further the cause of human rights in Nigeria. The organization submitted a shadow report to the UN Committee on Economic, Social and Cultural Rights, when Nigeria's compliance with the Covenant was under discussion in May 1998.

Here, however, attention will shift to the organization's use of the World Bank Inspection Panel and the African Commission on Human and Peoples' Rights. SERAC turned to the Inspection Panel, because no other remedy was available to test the legitimacy of the Bank's support of a controversial project in Lagos. The Charter-based UN human rights bodies did get involved with the Nigerian government's treatment of the Ogoni, but the African Commission appeared to be the treaty-monitoring body best equipped to deal with an essentially collective complaint on behalf of an entire ethnic community.

Lagos slum dwellers, Doba residents and the World Bank Inspection Panel

It is worth briefly summarizing the World Bank's position on human rights. The Bank denies that it is bound by human rights *law*. On the other hand, the Bank is a development institution that subscribes to a comprehensive approach to development, which includes a human rights dimension. Since the 1990s, the Bank has been willing to finance human rights projects and, in addition, it has adopted a number of internal instructions (currently called 'operational policies') that touch upon human rights issues. World Bank staff are obliged to take into account the instructions when deciding on funding. Only one of the policies – the operational directive on indigenous peoples (see below) – explicitly refers to human rights.

Since 1993, the Bank has accepted that it is directly accountable to people affected by Bank-funded projects when it fails to comply with its own policies. Direct accountability of an intergovernmental organization to populations is unusual. In traditional international law, intergovernmental organizations are accountable only to their member-states. The member-states, and not the international organization, are accountable to the people. The Bank's acceptance of direct accountability implies recognition of the important impact of Bank financing on the quality of life of affected people. The entry point opened up to adversely affected communities is the World Bank Inspection Panel.[3]

The panel hears requests for inspection of a Bank-supported project presented to it by an affected party demonstrating

That its rights or interests have been or are likely to be directly affected by an action or omission of the Bank as a result of a failure of the Bank to follow its operational policies and procedures with respect to the design, appraisal and/or implementation of a project financed by the Bank (including situations where the

Bank is alleged to have failed in its follow-up on the borrower's obligations under loan agreements with respect to such policies and procedures) provided in all cases that such failure has had, or threatens to have, a material adverse effect.

The Inspection Panel can test Bank compliance only with its own operational policies. It investigates whether staff complied with the rules in specific cases. The panel does not test whether or not Bank action violated international law. That does not prevent people, however, from arguing that the harm they suffered consisted of human rights violations. The panel takes up human rights violations *to the extent that* they result from an infringement of Bank rules.

One current operational directive explicitly uses human rights terminology. Operational Directive 4.20 on Indigenous Peoples states:[4]

The Bank's broad objective towards indigenous people, as for all the people in its member countries, is to ensure that the development process fosters full respect for their dignity, human rights, and cultural uniqueness. More specifically, the objective at the center of this directive is to ensure that indigenous peoples do not suffer adverse effects during the development process, particularly from Bank-financed projects, and that they receive culturally compatible social and economic benefits.[5]

The operational directive has a broad personal scope, including all 'social groups with a social and cultural identity distinct from the dominant society that makes them vulnerable to being disadvantaged in the development process'.

The panel procedure is administrative rather than judicial in nature, allowing an important role for the board in the different stages of the procedure. Panel reports are recommendatory only. The board decides both on whether or not to allow an investigation after the panel's preliminary eligibility report, and on remedial action after completion of the panel's full investigation. Board decisions are potentially a source of legal obligation for Bank staff, while the Inspection Panel's findings are not. In practice, the board never takes an express position on the findings of the Inspection Panel. The board never identifies a specific Bank practice as a violation of Bank operational policies, and even less as a violation of human rights. The board decides on action, not on law. Decisions on action after a panel investigation are 'case by case, tailor-made', and in response to action points proposed by management. At best, board decisions constitute an implicit endorsement of the panel's findings on non-compliance.

The Inspection Panel procedure does not provide for reparation by the Bank to persons adversely affected by Bank actions, nor does the Inspection Panel have a role in monitoring the implementation of the remedial action plan as approved by the board following an investigation. Clearly, the Inspection Panel is not a mechanism that allows holding the Bank responsible for complicity in human rights violations. But the investigations are instrumental in clarifying how the Bank affects human rights.

The aim of the 'Nigeria: Lagos drainage and sanitation' project was to improve the storm-water drainage system in parts of Lagos that suffered from regular inundation from heavy rains. The project involved the removal of a number of shelters built by the slum dwellers that intruded into the drainage right of way. The residents, only one of whom had a certificate of occupancy, were to be resettled and properly compensated. The World Bank (technically the International Development Association) approved the relevant credit on 17 June 1993.

Five days earlier, Nigeria's military ruler, Babangida, had organized presidential elections that were deemed to herald Nigeria's transition towards multiparty democracy. On 26 June 1993, however, President Babangida annulled the elections. A

149

military counter-coup ended the chaos that followed and brought General Abacha to power. Gross and systematic violations of human rights continued until Abacha's death on 8 June 1998. On 16 June 1998, SERAC filed the Lagos drainage and sanitation request.

SERAC argued that the Bank and the military government of Nigeria had failed to consult with affected communities 'in flagrant violation of the Bank's Operational Directive, the Constitution of the Federal Republic of Nigeria, the International Covenant on Economic, Social and Cultural Rights and other relevant international human rights instruments'. The demolition of homes and destruction of properties constituted a massive violation of the rights of victims to adequate housing, education, adequate standards of living, security of person, a healthy environment, food, health, work, respect of dignity inherent in a human being, freedom of movement, family life, water, privacy, information and the right to chose one's own residence. Specific allegations were made as to incidents involving police brutality and gender discrimination.

The Bank's management flatly denied that human rights violations had occurred. There was no evidence of police brutality in the context of the Bank-financed project; no gender discrimination had taken place; community leaders had not complained of human rights violations; there had been regular consultation. In short: 'The Bank-financed project had not violated anybody's rights.' On the other hand, management conceded that it did not have the resources to observe every activity that happened in the course of the project. The response repeatedly stressed that many of the alleged violations (such as forced evictions by heavily armed police) were not related to Bank-financed activities, and were thus the sole responsibility of Nigeria: 'In any case, the Bank does not have the authority to discipline officials of the Lagos State government.'

The Inspection Panel largely concurred with management on the lack of factual evidence, and considered that many of the claims were exaggerated or untrue. The panel did not recommend a full investigation to the board.[6] Nevertheless, the Inspection Panel did not hesitate to review and conclude on the issue of human rights violations in connection with the project. The panel criticized the Bank for overly relying on state officials to do the consultation with communities, and stated that much closer supervision should have been provided, while recognizing the financial constraints, and the division of responsibilities as agreed upon in the loan agreement. The panel acknowledged 'the concerns and the efforts of SERAC for exhibiting such courage in defending the rights of the affected people during the past regime in Nigeria'. The panel believed that its involvement had made it possible for the requesters to develop a better dialogue with IDA staff in the resolution of outstanding issues.

SERAC was disappointed. In its view, the panel relied too heavily on assurances given by the Lagos state government and the Bank that evicted slum dwellers would be adequately compensated. According to the organization, the project exacerbated the flood damage: 'Stagnant waste water now accumulates in open drainage channels that were never completed.'[7]

The handling of the Lagos drainage and sanitation project demonstrates the unease of the Bank in dealing with changing political circumstances. The Board of Executive Directors' approval of the project after election day but before the final results were made public can be seen as testimony to the Bank's traditional position that political circumstances are irrelevant to decisions on loans. The timing of the decision also deprived the Bank, however, of a chance to consider the impact of the annulment of the elections on the feasibility of project implementation and monitoring.

The continued ignorance of the political context on the part of Bank staff – as evidenced by their reliance on state officials who were part of a political system which showed with the utmost arrogance that it did not value political participation – indicates a real lack of sensitivity to the component of the project dealing with consultation and protection of evictees. The Bank's abandonment of the fulfilment of consultation requirements to its authoritarian partner is simply indefensible.

The panel's recommendation not to pursue the investigation was probably influenced by the fact that by the time the panel investigated the project the political pendulum had swung once again. The international community was keen to support a quick transition to democracy after Abacha's demise. Clearly, the inspectors exhibited a degree of confidence in the willingness of the new democracy to treat affected people properly, i.e. to compensate them in accordance with IDA policies. Later developments in other house demolition cases (discussed above) show that that confidence was not honoured.

In a different case, the Inspection Panel dealt at length with the human rights implications of the activities of the World Bank. The 'Chad–Cameroon petroleum and pipeline' project is the largest energy infrastructure development on the African continent, at an estimated total cost of US\$ 3.7 billion. It involves the drilling of 300 oil wells in the oil fields of the Doba region of southern Chad and the construction of a 1,100km-long export pipeline through Cameroon to an offshore loading facility. A consortium of private actors, consisting of Exxon Mobile (US, 40 per cent), Petronas (Malaysia, 35 per cent) and Chevron (US, 25 per cent) finances approximately 60 per cent of the project. In financial terms, the contribution of the World Bank group to the project is a minor one, but its commitment was essential in securing the support of other donors and private investors.

The board of the World Bank approved the project on 6 June 2000. On 22 March 2001, Ngarlejy Yorongar and more than 100 residents of the Doba area submitted a request for inspection of the Chad component of the project. Mr Yorongar is a member of parliament from the region who was also running as an opposition candidate in Chad's presidential elections, taking place in May 2001. Those making the request invoked the rights to life, to a healthy environment, to fair and equitable compensation, to resettlement not far from their native soil, to work, to respect for their customs and burial places, to social well-being, to public consultation. They argued that there had not been respect for human rights in Chad since President Déby took power and that massive violations of human rights had occurred in the production zone.

After an on-site visit in August, the Inspection Panel recommended an investigation on 17 September 2001.[8] The board approved the investigation on 1 October 2001. After another on-site visit, the panel sent its investigation report to the board on 17 July 2002.[9] On 12 September 2002 the board recorded its approval of the actions and next steps put forth by the Bank management in response to the panel's findings.[10]

Bank management argued that human rights violations were relevant to the Bank's work only if they had 'a significant direct economic effect on the project'. Management was of the view that this was not the case here: 'The Project can achieve its developmental objectives.'

The Inspection Panel took 'issue with Management's narrow view'. Ngarlejy Yorongar was jailed in 1998 for speaking out against the project, and again briefly detained and tortured shortly after the May 2001 presidential elections, while the request was pending with the Inspection Panel.[11] This background no doubt contributed to the panel's frustration with management's 'economic effects' approach. Relying explicitly on Amnesty International Annual Reports, the panel concluded that the human rights situation remained 'far from ideal': 'It raises questions about compliance with Bank operational policies, in particular those that relate to open and informed consultation, and it warrants renewed monitoring by the Bank.'

In an unprecedented move, the Bank published the remarks made by the chairman of the Inspection Panel, when he presented the investigation report to the board.[12] Inspection Panel chairman Ayensu further developed the human rights theme. The panel was convinced that the approach taken in the report, 'which finds human rights implicitly embedded in various policies of the Bank', was within the boundaries of the panel's jurisdiction. The chairman reiterated that the situation in Chad exemplified the need for the Bank to be more forthcoming about articulating its promotional role in human rights. He also invited the board to study the wider ramifications of human rights violations as they relate to the overall success or failure of policy compliance in future Bank-financed projects.

Public documents provide no evidence of a reply from the board to the chairman's call. The management action plan as adopted by the board in response to the panel investigation does not, however, address the concerns the panel raised about the effects on the project of the overall human rights situation in Chad. Consequently, it remains to be seen whether the panel's findings on human rights will have any impact on the conduct of Bank staff in the field.

Notwithstanding all the limitations of the procedure and the uncertainties about the effects of the reports, the creation of the Inspection Panel is an important step forward in enabling marginalized communities to question the legitimacy of an actor whose interventions are otherwise largely immune to legal challenges. The minimum effect of a panel investigation is to render visible groups that governments are eager to ignore. Inevitably, the political power of these groups on the domestic scene increases as a consequence of a panel investigation. That is an essential step to enable them to insist on protection of their rights in the long term. The direct human rights impact of panel decisions may be limited, but that should not deter social movements or human rights organizations from using the avenue.

Finally, even if the Bank still hangs on to the principled stance that it does not have human rights obligations, *in fact* the Bank has moved significantly on human rights, largely because it is now under detailed public scrutiny of non-governmental organizations via the Inspection Panel procedure. Thanks to the Inspection Panel procedure, discussion about the human rights responsibility of the Bank has moved from a conceptual discussion on the applicability of international human rights law, to a micro-level investigation of the human rights impact of specific Bank interventions on the lives of people who may otherwise be denied any international concern. In a number of cases, the panel investigations have contributed to bringing human rights home, i.e. to the communities that suffer injustice.

Ogoni and Awas Tingni

In March 1996, SERAC – still in its infancy at the time – together with the US-based Center for Economic and Social Rights filed a communication with the African Commission on Human and Peoples' Rights. The communication alleged that the military government had committed numerous violations of the African Charter in the context of oil exploitation activities in part of the Niger Delta inhabited by the Ogoni people. The state oil company was a majority shareholder in a consortium with the Shell Petroleum Development Corporation (SPDC) that exploited the resources in the area.

The conflict between the Ogoni, one of the many ethnic groups in the Niger Delta, and the military regime reached its peak in November 1995. At that time, the president of the Movement for the Survival of the Ogoni People (MOSOP), Ken Saro-Wiwa, and

Box 6.1 Ogoni Bill of Rights, 26 August 1990

In August 1990, the Ogoni people 'by general acclaim' adopted an Ogoni Bill of Rights, which was presented to the government in November of the same year. In the text, the Ogoni refer to themselves as a separate and distinct ethnic nationality. Towards the end of the Bill, the following demands are made of the Nigerian government:

That the Ogoni people be granted POLITICAL AUTONOMY to participate in the affairs of the Republic as a distinct and separate unit by whatever name called, provided that this Autonomy guarantees the following:

a) Political control of Ogoni affairs by Ogoni people.
b) The right to the control and use of a fair proportion of OGONI economic resources for Ogoni development.
c) Adequate and direct representation as of right in all Nigerian national institutions.
d) The use and development of Ogoni Languages in Ogoni territory.
e) The full development of Ogoni Culture.
f) The right to religious freedom.
g) The right to protect the OGONI environment and ecology from further degradation.

We make the above demand in the knowledge that it does not deny any other ethnic group in the Nigerian Federation their rights and that it can only conduce to peace, justice and fair play and hence stability and progress in the Nigerian nation.

We make the above demand in the belief that, as Obafemi Awolowo has written: 'In a true Federation, each ethnic group, no matter how small, is entitled to the same treatment as any other ethnic group, no matter how large.'

We demand these rights as equal members of the Nigerian Federation who contribute and have contributed to the growth of the Federation and have a right to expect full returns from that Federation.

eight of his colleagues were executed following a trial that was in clear violation of international human rights. The Ogoni were not the only group that suffered harm from the exploitation of natural resources in area. Ethnic conflict in Nigeria often revolves around control over natural resources, particularly because many of the resources are not located in or under lands owned or controlled by the ethnic groups that dominate the country's politics. Few members of the Yoruba, Ibo and Hausa-Fulani reside in the oil-rich Niger Delta (Omoroghe 2002: 554, 558). Ethnic conflicts over natural resources continue to date. In 2003 Human Rights Watch reported the killing of hundreds of people, the displacement of thousands, and the destruction of hundreds of properties at the hands of various actors in the Delta state.[13]

In the early 1990s, the Ogoni successfully captured the attention of international public opinion, raising awareness of their plight with a variety of international NGOs, working on environmental issues, minorities and indigenous peoples, and human rights. Clifford explains how MOSOP was ready to reframe its initial claims based on Ogoni autonomy (as in the Ogoni Bill of Rights reproduced in Box 6.1) in terms that were more attractive to organizations such as Greenpeace and Amnesty International. Support from the major international networks was dependent on identifying the issues in terms of environmental degradation, corporate accountability and abuses by Nigerian security forces (Clifford 2002: 139–44), rather than in terms of autonomy.

SERAC's complaint to the African Commission went largely unnoticed at the time, as numerous intergovernmental organizations, including the United Nations General Assembly, the Organization of African Unity, the Commonwealth and the European Union took centre-stage to express their dissatisfaction with Abacha's repressive practices. In 1997 the UN Commission on Human Rights appointed a Special Rapporteur on the situation of human rights in Nigeria, with a mandate to establish direct contacts with the authorities and the people of Nigeria.[14] The Special Rapporteur, however, was not allowed to visit the country until after Abacha's death in 1998.

Strategically, approaching the African Commission was not an obvious choice. Its record had not been impressive generally, and was particularly unimpressive in the areas touched upon by the communication (Agbakwa 2002: 193–4). It took the African Commission more than six years to consider the case.[15] In the course of the proceedings, the new Nigerian government even volunteered a statement to the Commission that 'there was no denying the fact that a lot of atrocities were and are still being committed by the oil companies in Ogoni Land and indeed in the Niger Delta area'. It did not take any political courage to condemn the defunct regime. In fact, the expression of thanks by the Commission in its report to the NGOs that brought the matter within its purview, and its comments on the usefulness of an *actio popularis*, 'which is wisely allowed under the African Charter', leave a somewhat sour taste.

The merit of the Commission's decision lies not in its contribution to reparation for abuses suffered, but in its revival of the African Charter. The Commission's application of the African Charter's unique provisions on peoples' rights is significant. Had SERAC not initiated the procedure with the Commission, the revival would have been postponed until some other non-governmental initiative materialized.

Throughout the report, the African Commission stresses the collective aspects of the violations, both by emphasizing the collective dimensions of the individual rights in the Charter, and by breathing life into the provisions dealing with collective rights.

The African Commission finds that Nigeria violated two collective rights, namely peoples' right to dispose freely of their wealth and natural resources (Article 21) and their right to inhabit a satisfactory environment favourable to their development (Article 24). On Article 21, the African Commission finds that

> The Government of Nigeria facilitated the destruction of the Ogoniland. Contrary to its Charter obligations and despite such internationally established principles, the Nigerian Government has given the green light to private actors, and the oil Companies in particular, to devastatingly affect the well-being of the Ogonis. By any measure of standards, its practice falls short of the minimum conduct expected of governments, and therefore, is in violation of Article 21 of the African Charter.[16]

On the different economic and social rights invoked by the authors of the communication, the general approach is that although these rights are framed as individual rights, in this case the Ogoni as a people are the victims. The resources belonging to the group should be respected, the report argues, as they are needed by the group. The right to housing – a right not explicitly mentioned in the African Charter, but read into the text by combining the rights to health, property and protection of family life – is violated by the practice of forced evictions, and these violations affect the Ogoni collectively. On the right to life, the African Commission states:

> Given the widespread violations perpetrated by the Government of Nigeria and by private actors (be it following its clear blessing

or not), the most fundamental of all human rights, the right to life has been violated. The Security forces were given the green light to decisively deal with the Ogonis, which was illustrated by the widespread terrorisations and killings. The pollution and environmental degradation to a level humanly unacceptable has made living in the Ogoni land a nightmare. The survival of the Ogonis depended on their land and farms that were destroyed by the direct involvement of the Government. These and similar brutalities not only persecuted individuals in Ogoniland but also the whole of the Ogoni Community as a whole.[17]

Finally, the African Commission emphasizes the uniqueness of the African Charter: 'Clearly, collective rights, environmental rights, and economic and social rights are essential elements of human rights in Africa. The African Commission will apply any of the diverse rights contained in the African Charter. It welcomes this opportunity to make clear that there is no right in the African Charter that cannot be made effective.'[18]

The Commission's adoption of a collective approach is facilitated by procedural requirements. Under the rules specific to the African Charter (and unlike other international and regional human rights mechanisms), the Commission is entitled to examine only individual cases that reveal the existence of a serious and massive violation of human and peoples' rights.

The report has far-reaching consequences for the exploitation of natural resources in multi-ethnic African societies that the Commission may or may not have intended.

Clearly, the Commission perceives of the Ogoni as a people under the African Charter. The text makes only sporadic use of the terms 'Ogoni people'[19] and 'people of Ogoniland',[20] but no sense can be made of the findings in Articles 21 and 24 unless the Ogoni are a people for the purposes of the Charter. The Commission's position that ethnic groups within states can claim the rights attributed to peoples in the African Charter is revolutionary. It goes against the view that African *states* have defended since independence. Their self-proclaimed aim was to build unity among the diverse ethnic communities that inhabited the countries fabricated by the colonial powers. In their view, peoples' rights could be exercised only by the population of the country as a whole, not by separate groups. The strategies pursued by the Nigerian government to achieve this aim had the disastrous result described in the Commission's report.

The African Commission's finding that resources first serve to satisfy the needs of the group they belong to, and that the Ogoni hold a right to dispose freely of their natural wealth and resources, also contrasts with the Nigerian constitution. In the constitution, the entire property and control of all minerals in Nigeria is vested in the government of the federation. The population of Nigeria as a whole enjoys the right to dispose freely of its natural wealth and resources, and the government has a duty to exercise this right in the population's interest. There is no doubt that the military government failed in exercising that duty properly *vis-à-vis* the Ogoni, and probably also *vis-à-vis* the large majority of its population.

The alternative open to the African Commission would have been to declare that in a multi-ethnic society the government's duty to manage natural resources in the public interest requires participation in the development of energy resources by the ethnic groups that face the environmental and social consequences of the exploitation, and entitles these groups to an equitable share in the revenues. Indeed, groups that face the burden of such exploitation should also share in the rewards, at the very least to the extent required to satisfy their basic needs. Such a decision would also have insisted on a radical change in Nigerian policies, but would perhaps have been less threatening to the continued existence of a state that has long been hovering on the brink of implosion.

The conceptual daring of the African Commission is tempered by its recommendations on the remedies the Nigerian state should offer. They amount to no more than 'a politely phrased request' (Bekker 2003: 131) to the current government to improve the situation. States do not have a legal obligation to implement African Commission reports. Publication is the only sanction.

Nevertheless, the Ogoni Report certainly sets the stage for the African Court on Human and Peoples' Rights. Once it is established, the Court will consider cases of human rights violations referred to it by the African Commission and states parties to the protocol and, where a state accepts such a jurisdiction, by individuals and non-governmental organizations. Unlike the African Commission, the African Court possesses the authority to issue a binding and enforceable decision on cases brought before it.

The emphasis of the African Commission on the African approach to human rights finds an echo in the judgment of the Inter-American Court of Human Rights in *Mayagna (Sumo) Awas Tingni Community v. Nicaragua*.[21] This case also involved exploitation of natural resources affecting an indigenous people.

In Africa, the notion of 'indigenous people' as a legal category is controversial. According to one author, the term is hardly used within Nigeria (Omoroghe 2002: 568). In Latin America, however, indigenous peoples have achieved widespread legal recognition in domestic legislation. ILO Convention no. 169 concerning indigenous and tribal peoples in independent countries (27 June 1989) offers the following description:

> Peoples in independent countries who are regarded as indigenous on account of their descent from the populations which inhabited the country, or a geographical region to which the country belongs, at the time of conquest or colonisation or the establishment of present state boundaries and who, irrespec-

tive of their legal status, retain some or all of their own social, economic, cultural and political institutions.

The Awas Tingni community, a group situated in Nicaragua's North Atlantic coastal region, initiated the proceedings with the assistance of the Indian Law Resource Center, a US-based NGO advocating the protection of indigenous peoples' human rights. The applicants claimed that Nicaragua had violated the rights of the indigenous community by granting concessions to a Korean timber company for logging on the community's traditional lands. The community had not been properly consulted, nor had its consent been obtained.

The Inter-American Court approached the issue from the angle of the (individual) rights to judicial protection and to property. Article 21 of the Inter-American Convention states: 'Everyone has the right to the use and enjoyment of his property. The law may subordinate such use and enjoyment to the interest of society.' The Court recalled that during the drafting history of the convention a reference to *private* property was deleted from the text. It then applied 'an evolutionary interpretation' (i.e. an innovative approach) to the provision in order to find that Article 21 also protected the communal property rights of indigenous communities. The Court clarified that these rights had nothing in common with individual property rights in a free-market economy:

Among indigenous peoples there is a communitarian tradition regarding a communal form of collective property of the land, in the sense that ownership of the land is not centered on an individual but rather on the group and its community. Indigenous groups, by the fact of their very existence, have the right to live freely in their own territory; the close ties of indigenous people with the land must be recognized and understood as the fundamental basis of their cultures, their spiritual life, their integrity, and their economic survival. For indigenous communities, relations to the land are not merely a matter of possession and production but a material and spiritual element which they must fully enjoy, even to preserve their cultural legacy and transmit it to future generations.[22]

The different character of indigenous communal rights did not matter. The protection offered by the Convention remained.

In order to determine what land was communal property, indigenous peoples' customary law needed to be taken into account. Indigenous law determined that *possession* of land sufficed for indigenous communities lacking real title.

The Court found that the members of the community had a communal property right to the lands they inhabited, but that the limits of the territory were unclear. This was due to a failure by the state to delimit and demarcate the territory. The Court ordered Nicaragua to remedy this failure within a maximum term of fifteen months. Until that time, the state was to abstain from carrying out or facilitating actions that affect the community.

The Court concluded that:

In light of article 21 of the Convention, the state has violated the right of the members of the Mayagna Awas Tingni Community to the use and enjoyment of their property, and that it has granted concessions to third parties to utilize the property and resources located in an area which could correspond, fully or in part, to the lands which must be delimited, demarcated, and titled.[23]

The Awas Tingni judgment is a fine example of how a regional court – through an acknowledgement of the relevance of the customary law of the indigenous group – can allow for plurality within a treaty. The content of the right to property varies according to the definition given to the right by the relevant group. The local concept of communal property gives specific meaning to the abstract norm in the regional treaty, and receives protection at the regional level, when infringement by the state occurs. By offering protection at the regional level, the Court simultaneously speaks to other indigenous peoples on the continent that may find themselves in a similar predicament.

The opportunities that exist within the human rights regime to accommodate plurality – if only the relevant institutions are willing to allow for it – become even clearer when the decisions in the Ogoni and Awas Tingni cases are read together. The legal approaches of the Inter-American Court and the African Commission could not be more different. One relies on the collective right of an ethnic group; the other on a communal concept specific to indigenous peoples. Nevertheless, both decisions concern what is in essence a similar conflict, namely a dispute between a state and an ethnic community over the exploitation of natural resources in an area claimed by the community. Both do so by reference to the human rights framework. It is not evident that the Latin American approach would transfer well to Africa, or vice versa. The Awas Tingni and the Ogoni – the primary authors of these new legal developments in peoples' rights – also use different concepts in framing their claims, although again they both rely on the broad category of human rights. The governments they face vary in their willingness to accommodate these claims, and thus contribute to the difference in approach as well. Taken together, the cases testify to the potential of human rights to combine rules that apply regionally or globally with diverse approaches growing out of the experiences of local communities.

If applied properly, global human rights do not stand in the way of plurality.

Still, it is useful to preserve the common language of human rights, particularly in the context of economic globalization. The use of this common language helps to identify common causes of violations that are not domestic or regional, but global. It is worth recalling that in both the Ogoni and Awas Tingni cases, state human rights violations are driven by the desire of the state to offer favourable conditions to foreign investors.

The companies themselves escape the regional bodies' legal scrutiny, because the regional bodies have no competence under the treaties that establish them to investigate the direct responsibility of private actors. Nevertheless, in the field of corporate human rights responsibility, new, if somewhat peculiar avenues, are opening up as well.

Wiwa v. Shell

Corporate responsibility is another area where there is a definite need for further development of the human rights regime. As discussed earlier, current global human rights systems offer little protection against human rights abuses by companies, except very indirectly via the duty of the state to protect against abuse by third parties. The same situation applies at the level of the regional institutions. That leaves only two possible tracks: the application of domestic law, either of the home country of the company or of the host country, or not applying law at all but striving towards compliance by using non-legal means such as self-regulation by the companies (introducing human rights as a corporate standard of excellence, particularly for global companies), or public opinion campaigns focusing on naming and shaming.

The most significant developments in establishing direct corporate responsibility for human rights have occurred through the extraterritorial application of the domestic law of the home state to the activities of the company in the country where it operates.

The action now moves to New York, where a case is heard that relates to the same events discussed in the African Commission's Ogoni report. The stage is a district court. SERAC no longer travels with us. Other actors play leading roles: the relatives of

Ken Saro-Wiwa and Blessing Kpuinen, who were executed by the Abacha government, and a woman who remains anonymous but alleges that she was beaten and shot by government troops while protesting about the bulldozing of her crops in preparation for a Shell pipeline. Two US-based NGOs, Earth Rights International and the Center for Constitutional Rights, support the plaintiffs with the assistance of public interest law firms.

The plaintiffs accuse the Royal Dutch Petroleum Company and Shell Transport and Trading Company (incorporated and headquartered in the Netherlands and the United Kingdom respectively) of complicity in the November 1995 hangings and other human rights violations related to the Ogoni conflict. The former head of the Nigerian subsidiary of Shell, Brian Anderson (a UK citizen who claims he resides in Hong Kong and France), is also charged. Anderson was allegedly involved in person in facilitating human rights violations. Only one of the plaintiffs resides in the United States. None of the main actors is an American national.

The histories of Shell and Nigeria are intertwined. Shell came to the territory in 1938 when the colonial power granted it a concession over the entire mainland of Nigeria. Shell was the only concessionaire, and 'therefore was able to explore at its convenience and to select acreage of its choice until 1962, by which time it retained 15,000 square miles of the original concession area' (Omorogbe 2002: 552). Today, Shell remains the largest concessionaire, and maintains by far the largest onshore operations in the country. It has traditionally received strong backing from the Nigerian government.

Why is the Saro-Wiwa case heard in New York? The events took place in Nigeria. The company is not American, nor are the plaintiffs. It is not self-evident that a US court is the most appropriate court to hear the claim. Two pieces of American legislation are relevant. The first is the Alien Tort Claims Act (ATCA) (a law originally adopted in 1789) providing that US district courts 'shall have original jurisdiction of any civil action by an alien for a tort only, committed in violation of the law of nations or a treaty of the United States'. In 1992, the US Congress passed a complement to this law, the Torture Victims Protection Act, which the plaintiffs invoke in addition to ATCA, in the case against Anderson. The Torture Victims Protection Act enables US or foreign nationals to bring a civil action against a person who, acting under 'actual or apparent authority or colour of law, of any foreign nation', subjects an individual to torture or extra-judicial killing.

Both laws deal with torts, not criminal law. They apply extra-territorially, i.e. to events outside the United States. Nevertheless, for US courts to be competent, sufficient factors are needed to connect the case to the United States. In the case against Shell, this issue had already been decided by a US Court of Appeals (discussed at length in Fellmeth 2002). An appeal by the defendants to the Supreme Court was unsuccessful. On 14 September 2000, the Court of Appeals held that US courts had jurisdiction, primarily on the grounds that the United States had an interest in furnishing a forum to litigate claims of violations of the international standards of the law of human rights. The Torture Victims Protection Act instituted a policy favouring receptivity by US courts of this type of claims. Torture in a foreign country was US business, and not just of concern to bodies monitoring international standards.

The decision did not please everyone in the United States. In May 2003 the US Department of Justice filed a friend-of-the-court brief in a similar case on the alleged involvement of Unocal in human rights violations in Burma (compare De Feyter 2001b: 94–7). The Ministry of Justice argued that the ATCA law should not be applied to human rights cases at all, but only to breaches of international law as defined in 1789, when the law was adopted. Lobby groups linked to US business campaign for the US Congress to amend or repeal the ATCA law, or to give the Executive Branch 'veto power' over the adjudication of particular legal claims.[24]

Even from a perspective favourable to the establishment of corporate responsibility for human rights, there may be concerns about US courts taking up a role more befitting global institutions. Undeniably, 'extraterritoriality is linked to the recent history of American power' (Muchlinski 1999: 109). It takes a superpower to extend the reach of its domestic legislation across the globe, even if in this instance that legislation reflects international law. In a different case dealing with the same legislation, but not with corporate responsibility, the US Supreme Court urged caution:

> Still, there are good reasons for a restrained conception of the discretion a federal court should exercise in considering a new cause action of this kind. Accordingly, we think courts should require any claim based on the present-day law of nations to rest on a norm of international character accepted by the civilized world and defined with a specificity comparable to the features of the 18th-century paradigms we have recognized. [25]

According to the Supreme Court, this test did not affect the authority of US courts to entertain claims based on torture and extra-judicial killing, but the test was fatal to the claim at hand, which was based on an alleged customary rule prohibiting 'a single illegal detention of less than a day, followed by the transfer of custody to lawful authorities and prompt arraignment'.

There is an element of supremacy in the ease with which US judges dismiss the appropriateness of domestic courts, particularly in developing countries. Obviously, trial in the host country is not an option if the courts are not independent or impartial. Burma offers a case in point. Even during military rule, however, Nigerian judges decided many oil exploitation-related compensation cases against Shell (Freynas 1999). It is true that none of these cases involved high politics in the way the Ogoni case does. In the latest 2002 judgment on the Saro-Wiwa case,[26] the US judge argues that although political conditions in Nigeria have improved since 1995, 'Nigerian courts remain an uncertain forum for justice'. The only reported source for the assessment is a 2000 US State Department annual country report on human rights practices. When Anderson argues that the exercise of juris-diction by a US court would infringe Nigerian sovereignty, the judge holds that the problem does not arise because the military regime responsible for the alleged torts has been replaced by a democracy, and consequently any findings of improprieties should be consonant rather than at odds with the present posi-tion of the Nigerian government. The two findings are somewhat contradictory. Surely, if the current government of Nigeria is democratic, it will not interfere with the course of justice. And if damages were awarded to victims of oil exploitation under military rule, then surely the same should be possible in a politi-cal climate that is more victim-friendly? Obviously, plaintiffs will receive higher amounts of reparation in the United States if their claim is granted there. So far none of the ATCA claims against corporations has led to a finding of liability on the corporation's behalf, so the outcome is unsure. But even if reparation were to be granted, the preferable solution may well be to locate the basis for the claims, and thus the legitimacy of human rights, in the societies where the violations take place (Mutua 2002: 81). In that respect, it is a pity that a distant court should decide the issue.

In order to establish corporate liability, plaintiffs need to show that the company was acting 'under colour of law'. The latter test requires that 'joint action' between the relevant state and the company is shown. Private actors are considered state actors if they are wilful participants in a joint action with the state or its agents. A company's presence in a zone of human rights abuses is not sufficient, nor does merely doing business with a repressive government lead to corporate liability under the legislation. In the Saro-Wiwa case, however, the judge was satisfied that the alleged facts demonstrated a substantial degree of cooperative action between the corporate defendants and the Nigerian government in the alleged violations of international law. The judge also agreed that the plaintiffs had alleged conduct that, if proven, would violate international human rights. Consequently, the trial has now moved to the so-called 'discovery phase', allowing defence lawyers to interview Anderson as well as other Shell employees to gather evidence.

In summary, clearly, new developments are taking place in different parts of the human rights regime that suggest an adjustment of the system to globalization. These developments include the opening up of new avenues for marginalized communities to test the accountability of important actors, including the World Bank and transnational corporations. There is some evidence that the human rights regime has the capacity to come to terms with a system of international relations that moves into the direction of multi-level governance.

Part of the battle must be fought within the human rights community itself. The decisions of human rights institutions reviewed in this chapter go in the general direction proposed in this book. At least, the chapter confirms that human rights are a living instrument, and thus have the potential to provide protection against the adverse consequences of the current model of globalization.

Notes

1 Article 15, 4d, Asian Human Rights Charter (17 May 1998), a peoples' charter declared in Kwangju, South Korea.

2 Universal Declaration on the Rights of Peoples, adopted in Algiers on 4 July 1976.

3 Resolution no. 93–10 of the Executive Directors establishing the

Inspection Panel for the IBRD (22 September 1993) and Resolution no. 93–6 for the IDA (22 September 1993). At the occasion of the tenth anniversary of the panel, the World Bank published a useful book (available from the Bank free of charge) presenting an overview of the panel's work: IBRD, *Accountability at the World Bank. The Inspection Panel 10 Years on* (Washington: IBRD 2003).

4 OD 4.20 (September 1991), par. 6.

5 OD 4.20 is under revision, and will be replaced by Operational Policy/Bank Procedure 4.10 on Indigenous Peoples. A consultation process with external stakeholders is currently ongoing. The most recent draft (23 March 2001), available from the World Bank website, moves the reference to human rights to the first paragraph of the text in a section entitled 'Overview'. The proposed text states, 'the broad objective of this policy is to ensure that the development process fosters full respect for the dignity, human rights and cultures of indigenous peoples, thereby contributing to the Bank's mission of poverty reduction and sustainable development'. Note the deletion of the reference to 'all the people', that appears in the current text.

6 Inspection Panel, Report and Recommendation on Request for Inspection on Nigeria: Lagos Drainage and Sanitation Project (6 November 1998).

7 See Morka, K. (1999), 'When Wilful Blindness Doesn't Cut It. Making the Case for World Bank Accountability to the Women in Lagos Slums', *Access Quarterly*, vol.1, no. 1 (1999): 5–10. *Access Quarterly* is the 'official magazine' of SERAC.

8 Inspection Panel, Report and Recommendation on Request for Inspection on Chad: Petroleum Development and Pipeline Project (17 September 2000).

9 Inspection Panel, Investigation Report on Chad–Cameroon Petroleum and Pipeline Project (17 July 2002).

10 See IBRD/IDA Press Release (18 September 2002), 'Chad–Cameroon Pipeline Project: Outcome of the Inspection Panel Investigation'. On 25 September 2002, the Center for the Environment and Development, a local NGO acting on behalf of people living alongside the pipeline, and a number of employees or former employees of the project, submitted a request for inspection on the Cameroon side of the project. The board again approved an investigation, in December 2002. The panel produced an investigation report on 2 May 2003. The board approved the management plan developed in response to the investigation report on 24 July 2003.

11 The Bank's president, James Wolfensohn, personally intervened to obtain the release of Mr Yorongar (see Inspection Panel,

Investigation Report on Chad–Cameroon Petroleum and Pipeline Project [17 July 2002], par. 213), by calling President Déby. Reportedly, the World Bank president was alerted by an NGO, not by Bank staff. See K. Horta, 'Rhetoric and Reality: Human Rights and the World Bank', *Harvard Human Rights Journal*, vol. 15 (Spring 2002): 236.

12 IBRD/IDA Press Release (18 September 2002), 'Chairman's Statement on Chad Investigation'. See also IBRD, *Accountability at the World Bank*, p. 97.

13 Human Rights Watch, *The Warri Crisis: Fuelling Violence*, vol. 15, no. 18(A) (November 2003).

14 UN Commission on Human Rights, Resolution 1997/53 (15 April 1997), adopted by 28 to 6 votes, with 19 abstentions. The reports of Special Rapporteur Soji Sorabjee are UN docs E/CN.4/1998/62 (16 February 1998) and E/CN.4/1999/36 (14 January 1999). The Commission terminated the mandate of the Special Rapporteur in 1999.

15 African Commission on Human and Peoples' Rights, Report re: Communication No. 155/96 (27 May 2002). For background on the delay, see Coomans 2003: 750.

16 African Commission on Human and Peoples' Rights, Report re: Communication no. 155/96 (27 May 2002), par. 58.

17 Ibid., par. 67.

18 Ibid., par. 68.

19 'The protection of the rights guaranteed in Articles 14, 16 and 18 (1) leads to the same conclusion. As regards the earlier right, and in the case of the Ogoni People, the Government of Nigeria has failed to fulfil these two minimum obligations' (ibid., par. 62).

20 Ibid., par. 69 and in the final operative paragraph.

21 Inter-American Court of Human Rights, *Mayagna (Sumo) Awas Tingni Community v. Nicaragua* (no. 79 (2001), Judgment of 21 August 2001. The *Arizona Journal of International and Comparative Law* published a special issue on the case in vol. 19, no. 1 (2002).

22 Ibid., par. 149.

23 Ibid., par. 153.

24 Useful background can be found at the website of the US-based Human Rights First NGO, on <www.humanrightsfirst.org>

25 US Supreme Court, *Sosa v. Alvarez-Machain et al.* (no. 03–339), Judgment of 29 June 2004.

26 US District Court for the Southern District of New York, *Wiwa et al. v. Royal Dutch Petroleum Co. et al.* (96 Civ. 8386 KMW), Judgment of 28 February 2002.

7 | The added value of human rights

Human rights scholarship often takes specific rights as the starting point of analysis. Books are written on the prohibition of torture or the right to food. Human rights mechanisms are regularly attached to a specific prohibition or right: a Special Rapporteur investigates the right to health; treaty-monitoring bodies draft a general comment on a specific treaty provision ... Human rights organizations equally tend to identify with one or more rights. FIAN focuses on the right to food, and contemporary forms of slavery define what the Anti-Slavery Society is about. As a result, issues are taken up to the extent that they are relevant to the relevant right. If the scope of the right does not cover aspects of an issue, or does not cover the issue at all, it falls outside the ambit of the research, or the remit of the institution. Much intellectual effort and internal debate goes into determining exactly how far a right extends. This test decides whether an organization takes action or not, or whether a subject can safely be ignored in a PhD.

Development practitioners often have difficulty in understanding such a blinkered approach. Development, environmental and trade organizations prefer to work on an issue as a whole, and may be frustrated to discover that their human rights counterparts are not interested in subjects that the development practitioners deem at least as important. They fight poverty, the unequal distribution of land, debt reduction, the improvement of the living conditions of slum dwellers or of single parents, the sustainable exploitation of natural resources, the trade in agriculture, the international financial institutions, and so on, and approach the issues *as holistically as possible*. The human rights practitioners reduce reality to a normative framework that may be of overriding importance to them, but not necessarily to others. Even the languages differ. In the international human rights covenants, there is no human right not to be poor, no human right to land, no human right to debt relief. An organization working on these issues may query whether human rights have anything to offer. Similarly, many human rights organizations may feel that trade agreements are none of their business, since the agreements do not mention human rights. The terminological gap does not facilitate the forming of alliances, and yet alliances are essential if the NGOs are to stand any chance of realizing their agenda in the face of important adverse forces.

From a human rights perspective, developing a 'human rights approach' rather than a focus on specific rights can narrow the gap. This approach takes issues as defined in the development, peace, trade and environmental agenda as a starting point, and then demonstrates how human rights are relevant. That still may not mean that all aspects can be covered meaningfully from a human rights angle, but a conscious effort is made to interpret and develop human rights in such a way that they are as relevant as possible to the environmental, peace and development agendas. The approach recognizes that there is a need to associate the human rights agenda with major global issues.

This chapter applies such an approach to a number of issues that have emerged in the context of the international debate on globalization. The perspective taken here reflects the 'ideal' approach described in Chapter 2 under the heading 'Increasing the relevance of human rights'. Each of the four sections below aims to indicate how a human rights approach adds value to the issue at hand. Different aspects of human rights figure more or less prominently depending on the issue. The sections deal with intellectual property, microcredit, privatization and agrarian reform.

175

Intellectual property rights protect the commercial interests of pharmaceutical companies that develop new drugs. The World Trade Organization requires from its member-states that this protection is effective. Human rights protect human life, and demand affordable access to essential drugs. In a nutshell, the practical implications of a human rights approach are as follows:

- domestic legislation on the protection of intellectual property rights should fully take into account the state's international human rights obligations
- pharmaceutical companies should respect human rights, and be accountable if they do not
- human rights law prevails over international trade law
- WTO disputes should be settled in conformity with international human rights law

Microcredit provides those living in extreme poverty with capital in order to start a small business. Microcredit initiatives and human rights share the same target group; there is no inherent contradiction between these approaches. Nevertheless, a human rights analysis demonstrates the limitations of many existing microcredit initiatives. Often, the initiatives accept poverty as a fact of life. A human rights approach, on the other hand, investigates whether poverty results from the conscious decisions of governments or of important economic actors. The analysis of the political and economic context is crucial in a human rights approach. The recipients of microcredit are not mere beneficiaries; they hold rights. Microcredit initiatives should therefore include an analysis of the behaviour of duty holders, and encourage borrowers to insist on justice. If that dimension is lacking, it is unlikely that marginalized communities will be emancipated from poverty, with the occasional exception of a successful individual entrepreneur.

A human rights approach to the *privatization of essential services* insists on active involvement by the state in ensuring that levels of protection remain guaranteed when the responsibility for the delivery of the service is handed over to a private operator. Private operators should respect human rights and be accountable to individuals and communities when they do not.

In the area of *agrarian reform*, human rights practitioners insist on access to productive resources for the landless, because without access to land the rural poor have little chance of procuring for themselves the basic amenities to which they are entitled under human rights law. At the same time, the experiences of the rural poor should inform the further development of the normative content of human rights. Human rights need to respond to the reality of what it means to be poor in a village that no public authority cares about. The experiences of the rural poor differ in different countries, and so the human rights response needs to allow for a degree of plurality within the context of the general norms set at the global level.

Intellectual property and pharmaceuticals

Knowledge is made subject to property in order to reward intellectual labour. Intellectual property protection encourages inventors and creators by providing them with benefits for their creativity. They reward the author for writing the book in your hand.

Intellectual property rights are divided into a number of groups such as patents, copyrights, trademark and industrial designs. Patents protect knowledge that is applicable to industry or other economic activities. An idea is considered worthy of patent if it is new, not obvious, and of practical use. The World Trade Organization provides the institutional framework for the main commercially-orientated international treaty on the issue, i.e. the Agreement on Trade-Related Aspects of Intellectual

Property Rights (TRIPs). As the WTO sees it, the aim of the basic patent right is to provide the patent owner with the legal means to prevent others from making, using or selling the new invention for a limited period of time, 'subject to a number of exceptions'.

The limitations and exceptions reflect the need to balance the interests of the producers of the idea with the interests of the users to benefit quickly from existing inventions and creations. The time limitation on the enjoyment of intellectual property rights by the owner reflects the 'weight of public or social benefit likely to result from the knowledge object's free dissemination' (May 2000: 65).

Human rights prioritize the impact of the protection of intellectual property on those marginalized in society. This is not the only non-economic concern that arises. An environmental approach may, for instance, look at the impact of the intellectual property regime on the preservation of biodiversity (Shiva 2001: 102). Certainly, a human rights approach does not exhaust the issue.

The tension between intellectual property rights and human rights is easily felt when patents are provided for pharmaceuticals. There are different aspects to this tenuous relationship. The commercial nature of intellectual property protection means that patents provide incentives for research directed towards 'profitable' diseases, but not for research into diseases that predominantly affect poor people. The Office of the High Commissioner for Human Rights has thus called for the creation of alternative incentives 'of comparable legitimacy and force to the TRIPs agreement' for research into neglected diseases that would enable states to fulfil their obligations under the right to health.[1] A very different issue of human rights concern is the patenting by transnational companies of the reproduction or adaptation of traditional knowledge held by local societies or indigenous peoples about the medicinal or nutritional effects of natural resources. Perhaps the most fundamental potential conflict between the intellectual property regime and human rights, however, stems from the latter's insistence that access to essential drugs is a human right. Does the human rights obligation to provide access trump trade law's insistence on reward for the inventor? Is there any credible accountability mechanism with which to decide the issue?

The market-friendly approach to the concurrence of trade law and human rights obligations allows the taking into account of human rights *to the extent determined by trade law*. The WTO intellectual property regime is self-contained. Only the TRIPs agreement provides the member-states with obligations and with the necessary means of defence and sanctions against possible abuse. Any human rights-related argument has to be brought under the treaty, which allegedly offers sufficient latitude to do so. Proponents of the market-friendly approach invariably argue that solutions for human rights problems need to be found *inside* the WTO system.

Certainly, efforts were made within the WTO to address the impact on health of the TRIPs agreement. On 14 November 2001 the WTO ministerial conference adopted the Doha Declaration on the TRIPs agreement and public health. The declaration clarified that the TRIPs agreement did not prevent members from taking measures to protect public health. The TRIPs agreement 'can and should be interpreted and implemented in a manner supportive of WTO members' right to protect public health and, in particular, access to medicines for all'. Each provision of the agreement was to be interpreted 'in the light of the object and purpose of the Agreement, as expressed, in particular in its objectives and principles'. The 'objectives and principles' of the TRIPs agreement recognize that intellectual property rights should be conducive to social and economic welfare (Article 7), and allow member-states to adopt measures necessary to protect public health and nutrition, provided that they are consistent with the agreement (Article 8). In short, the Doha Declaration illustrates to perfection what space the WTO system is willing to open up for human rights. On the insistence of a member-state, WTO provisions can be interpreted in the light of human rights law, but human rights law cannot be invoked to justify disregard of trade law obligations.

The Doha Declaration also confirms that each member-state has the right to determine what constitutes a national emergency or other circumstances of extreme urgency. Public health crises, including those related to HIV/AIDS, tuberculosis, malaria and other epidemics, could represent such circumstances. Article 31 of the TRIPs agreement enables governments, under certain conditions, to engage in compulsory licensing. Under such a scheme a patented drug can be produced without the consent of the patent owner. Normally, this can be done only after an attempt to obtain a voluntary licence on commercial terms has failed, but during a national emergency this condition is dispensed with.

The Doha Declaration did not modify the TRIPs agreement, but it did send the political message that a country plagued by a health crisis would be able to count on flexibility when it availed itself of the escape clause offered by the TRIPs agreement. The Doha Declaration recognized (in paragraph 6) that a problem remained for countries that had no capacity to produce pharmaceutical products, as a compulsory licence can be used only for the domestic market and not for export. So, on 30 August 2003, the WTO General Council adopted yet another decision 'on the implementation of paragraph 6 of the Doha Declaration' which, under complicated conditions, allowed a waiver from the TRIPs agreement to enable countries to export generic drugs under compulsory licences to countries with no or inadequate manufacturing capacity. The system under the 2003 decision is temporary, so there are, currently, ongoing negotiations about turning the waiver into a real amendment to the TRIPs agreement, thus ensuring that the settlement becomes permanent.

WTO proponents submit the declaration and the decision as evidence of that organization's willingness to consider the human rights impact of intellectual property rules, even if both texts carefully avoid all use of human rights language. No doubt the isolationist track on which the WTO departed when it was decided to separate the WTO from the UN system has been abandoned to some extent. From a human rights perspective, however, the offer of a human-rights-friendly interpretation of trade rules remains unsatisfactory, for exactly the same reasons trade lawyers refute limitations not allowed by trade law. The International Covenant on Economic, Social and Cultural Rights allows limitations on rights 'solely for the purpose of promoting the general welfare in a democratic society', not for the purpose of promoting the private interests of those holding intellectual property rights under the WTO regime.

Article 12 of the International Covenant on Economic, Social and Cultural Rights does not explicitly state that access to essential drugs is a human right. The UN Committee on Economic, Social and Cultural Rights, has, however, clarified the core obligations pertaining to the right to health in its relevant general comment. As a core obligation, state parties need to ensure the satisfaction of, at the very least, minimum essential levels of the rights in the Covenant. For the right to health, these core obligations include the obligation 'to provide essential drugs, as from time to time defined under the WHO Action Programme on Essential Drugs'.[2] The WHO last revised its model list on essential medicines in April 2003. The list defines essential medicines as those that satisfy the priority healthcare needs of the population. According to the World Health Organization, essential medicines should be available within the context of functioning health systems at all times in adequate amounts, in the appropriate dosage forms, with assured quality and adequate information, and at a price the individual and the community can afford. In stark contrast, 'in December 2002, only 5% of the estimated five and a half million people living with HIV and AIDS were getting the antiretroviral drugs they needed to save their lives' (Sleap 2004: 153).

It is worth mentioning at this point that Article 15 of the Covenant recognizes both the right of everyone 'to enjoy the benefits of scientific progress' and the right 'to benefit from the protection of moral and material interests resulting from any scientific, literary or artistic production of which he is the author'. But as Chapman explains, intellectual property conceptualized as a human right differs fundamentally from its treatment as an economic interest: 'From a human rights perspective [...] the rights of the creator are not absolute, but are conditional on contributing to the common good and welfare of the society' (Chapman 2002: 315). The UN Committee on Economic, Social and Cultural Rights agrees: 'Ultimately, intellectual property is a social product and has a social function. The end which intellectual property protection should serve is the objective of human well-being, to which international human rights instruments give legal expression.'[3] Obviously, in a perfect world, conflicts between trade law and human rights would not happen if states took full account of human rights during the drafting process of trade agreements. In its general comment on the right to health, the UN Committee on ESC Rights establishes that a state violates its obligation to respect the right to health if it fails 'to take into account its legal obligations regarding the right to health when entering into bilateral and multilateral agreements with other states, international organizations and other entities, such as multinational corporations'.[4] The general comment represents one attempt to adjust existing state obligations under the human rights treaties to the new context brought about by global trade rules.

Clearly, it should not be taken for granted that states will always be consistent in observing their human rights obligations in the whole realm of their international relations, including at the time of trade negotiations. The important question of the hierarchy in respect of human rights obligations and trade law obligations thus remains firmly on the table. For the UN Sub-Commission on the Promotion and Protection of Human Rights, the answer is clear. The sub-commission has reminded all governments, confronted with apparent conflicts between the TRIPs agreement and international human rights law, of the primacy of human rights obligations over economic policies and agreements.[5]

The statement reproduced in Box 7.1 argues eloquently why it should be common sense for human rights entitlements to take precedence in cases of conflict with intellectual property rights. Common sense, however, does not always prevail in international law.

The issues of hierarchy among treaties dealing with related, but not identical, subject matter, or of hierarchy between treaties and custom are notoriously difficult. Article 53 of the 1969 Vienna Convention on the law of treaties may provide a way out. According to the provision, a treaty is void when it conflicts with a peremptory norm of general international law. This is a norm 'accepted and recognized by the international community of states as a whole as a norm from which no derogation is permitted'. The prohibition of gross and systematic violations of human rights arguably falls within that category of peremptory norms. Consequently, a convincing legal argument can be made that the protection offered to patent holders of pharmaceutical products under the TRIPs agreement should yield whenever it

Box 7.1 UN Committee on Economic, Social and Cultural Rights, 'Statement on Human Rights and Intellectual Property', UN doc. E/C.12/2001/15 (14 December 2001), par. 6

The fact that the human person is the central subject and primary beneficiary of human rights distinguishes human rights, including the right of authors to the moral and material interests in their works, from legal rights recognized in intellectual property systems. Human rights are fundamental, inalienable and universal entitlements belonging to individuals, and in some situations groups of individuals and communities. Human rights are fundamental as they derive from the human person as such, whereas intellectual property rights derived from intellectual property systems are instrumental, in that they are a means by which States seek to provide incentives for inventiveness and creativity from which society benefits. In contrast with human rights, intellectual property rights are generally of a temporary nature, and can be revoked, licensed or assigned to someone else. While intellectual property rights may be allocated, limited in time and scope, traded, amended and even forfeited, human rights are timeless expressions of fundamental entitlements of the human person. Whereas human rights are dedicated to assuring satisfactory standards of human welfare and well being, intellectual property regimes, although they traditionally provide protection to individual authors and creators, are increasingly focused on protecting business and corporate interests and investments. Moreover, the scope of protection of the moral and material interests of the author provided for under article 15 of the Covenant does not necessarily coincide with what is termed intellectual property rights under national legislation or international agreements.

results in gross and systematic violations of the human right to have access to essential medicines.

Whether such an argument would be allowed by the WTO dispute settlement system is yet another matter. According to the WTO understanding governing the settlement of disputes, the dispute settlement system 'serves to preserve the rights and obligations of Members under the covered agreements, and to clarify the existing provisions of those agreements in accordance with customary rules of interpretation of public international law' (Article 3). The provision also states that the dispute settlement bodies cannot add to or diminish the rights and obligations provided in the covered agreements. This suggests that the dispute settlement bodies should not move far beyond a textual interpretation of the covered WTO agreements. The provisions on the composition of the panels and the appellate body stress knowledge of trade law and practice as a qualification for members, but require no knowledge or expertise in any other field of international law or practice.

It is unlikely that the dispute settlement bodies will set aside WTO law for the sake of recognizing the primacy of human rights norms. Oxfam has argued that relevant experts such as health professionals should be appointed to dispute settlement panels and that joint panels with other organizations such as the World Health Organization (WHO) should be set up when disputes have a significant non-trade dimension, but none of these proposals has been taken up in the current debates on the reform of the dispute settlement system.

In addition, the dispute settlement understanding requires that member-states have recourse to the rules and procedure of the understanding 'when [they] seek the redress of a violation of obligations or other nullification or impairment of benefits under the covered agreements or an impediment to the attainment of any objective of the covered agreements' (Article 23). The provision appears to require that WTO members use *only* the WTO settlement system for disputes involving WTO treaties.

Nevertheless, room for manoeuvre still exists at the domestic level. The TRIPs agreement does not replace domestic law. The agreement imposes important constraints on decision-making by WTO member-states in the area of intellectual property rights, but the state is still entitled to produce domestic legislation on the issue (Randeria 2003: 7). Given the political will, governments can still take protective measures *vis-à-vis* vulnerable groups. Domestic courts too can rely on constitutional human rights provisions and interpret them in the light of the general comment on the right to health to stop any interpretation of intellectual property rights that infringes on access to essential medicines.

The Supreme Court in Argentina has reportedly upheld a domestic law obliging the state to deliver HIV medicines to all people potentially affected (COHRE 2003: 64). In India, the courts have taken an ambivalent attitude towards the protection of the human rights of persons living with HIV/AIDS. India is under an obligation to implement fully the TRIPs agreement by 2005. Krishnan queries the consequences for patients presently receiving low-priced AIDS medication from non-TRIPs-compliant pharmaceutical companies. The author reports that HIV activists fear that once the agreement takes effect, the judiciary will do little to ensure that the needs of these individuals are met (Krishnan 2003: 817). Clearly, the Indian government and the Indian courts should avail themselves of the legal argument that under international and constitutional law human rights protection prevails.

Examples from South Africa are inspiring. In a case initiated by the Treatment Action Campaign, the South African Constitutional Court found that undue restrictions on the provision in public health institutions of Nevirapine, an anti-retroviral drug combating mother-to-child HIV transmission at birth, violated constitutional provisions on access to healthcare services and the rights of children whose parents could ill afford to provide such access (Magaisa 2003). The Court explicitly referred to South Africa's obligations in the International Covenant on Economic, Social and Cultural Rights. Nevirapine figures on the current WHO model list of essential medicines. An earlier 1998 South African court case which attracted wide international attention involved a suit brought by an umbrella body in South Africa representing the multinational pharmaceutical industry (cf. Sleap 2004: 165) challenging the validity of a South African Act allowing, inter alia, parallel importation of patented medications, drug price control and mandatory generic substitution of off-patented medicines. The Treatment Action Campaign intervened as a friend of the Court, and argued that the law did not infringe the TRIPs agreement but, even if it did, the government's obligations under the South African Constitution trumped its obligations under TRIPs. Médecins Sans Frontières organized a worldwide campaign and collected 250,000 signatures for a petition calling on the pharmaceutical companies to drop the case. In the face of international pressure, the companies withdrew from the action in 2001 and agreed to pay the legal costs of the South African government.

The case shows that litigation strategies will often need to be combined with other types of action in order to achieve success. If the human rights movement enjoys one comparative advantage over the pharmaceutical companies, it is its capacity to mobilize international public opinion.

One final point. In its statement on human rights and intellectual property, the UN Committee on ESC Rights also states: 'A human rights approach to intellectual property requires that all actors are held to account for their obligations under international human rights law, specifically with regard to the adoption, interpretation and implementation of intellectual property systems.'[6]

The focus of this section on the tension between trade human rights law has perhaps obscured the debate on the direct human rights responsibilities of pharmaceutical companies. Corporate actors were the driving forces behind the establishment of the TRIPs regime (May 2000: 72; Shiva 2001: 96), but remain invisible in the WTO dispute settlement system. Only member-states can be held accountable. The issue of corporate responsibility simply cannot be raised. This is another reason why developing a human rights approach to TRIPs is important. Such an approach assists actors who do not enjoy the welcoming attitude the WTO extends to groups defending corporate interests to restore a semblance of balance in international relations.

In conclusion, a human rights approach to intellectual property does not accept the tunnel vision imposed by the trade norms and dispute settlement system. It measures the protection of intellectual property rights against the human rights of marginalized communities, and the attainment of adequate standards of living. It insists on the responsible behaviour of both governments and pharmaceutical companies, and therefore on the availability of dispute settlement systems (such as domestic constitutional courts) competent to deal with the issue comprehensively, i.e. to enforce the responsibility of all relevant actors under a system of law that is not limited to trade rules.

Microcredit

The year 2005 is the International Year of Microcredit,[7] the final year of the campaign, launched at the Microcredit Summit (Washington, DC, 2–4 February 1997), aiming to reach 100 million of the world's poorest families, and especially the women of those families, with credit for self-employment and other financial and business services. The Declaration and Plan of Action adopted at the Washington summit defines microcredit thus: 'Microcredit programs extend small loans to poor people for self-employment projects that generate income, allowing them to care for themselves and their families.'

From a human rights perspective, helping poor people to generate an income for themselves is obviously important. Income provides for some of the resources needed to fulfil human rights, and avoids dependency on the intervention of other actors. It could well be argued that, under the International Covenant on Economic, Social and Cultural Rights, states have a duty to provide the legislative and economic environment that enables poor people to self-provide for their rights as much as possible. The question is, however, whether the provision of credit is sufficient to improve fundamentally the human rights situation of borrowers.

The targeted beneficiaries of microcredit programmes are people who remain outside the reach of the conventional banking system, because commercial providers of credit refuse to lend to the poor, primarily because they have no collateral in the form of property to pledge for the loan. In rural areas, those typically selected will be landless. The alternative bank guarantee is provided through peer-group control. The collateral is 'social'. Lending in most cases is to an individual, but the group to which she belongs shares responsibility for appropriate use of the loan and, under some schemes, for ensuring repayment. The cost of individual default is high since non-repayment of one member may bar any future loans to the other members of the group. Individuals are always part of a group of borrowers, usually neighbours or members of the same community. The selection of loan projects proposed for funding is a collective decision. Loans are not given for consumption, but to subsidize the setting up of a business. The providers of the credit – the micro-finance institutions – may be non-governmental, semi-commercial or even public actors.

Microcredit is connected to economic globalization. It has

certainly become a global venture. There are thousands of micro-credit organizations operating worldwide.[8] These organizations network and set up activities outside their country of origin. One of the main Bangladesh NGOs engaged in micro-finance, BRAC (Bangladesh Rural Advancement Committee), currently runs a micro-finance programme in Afghanistan. In addition, although microcredit may have started as a domestic non-governmental initiative, the donor community and the international financial institutions picked up the strategy quickly, and now offer generous support. Anderson even suggests that, given the current origin of the funding for microcredit, the governmental agencies of the developed countries are the driving force behind many of the programmes, with the micro-finance institutions acting as intermediaries *vis-à-vis* the local society (Anderson 2002: 110). On its website, the Grameen Bank nevertheless declares with some pride that it last received an instalment of donor funds in 1998. In any case, the variety in institutional set-ups of microcredit institutions once again raises intricate questions of how downward accountability *vis-à-vis* the beneficiaries is ensured.

Substantively, microcredit is an instrument for facilitating access to the market for the poor; it is a market-friendly device. The strategy contributes to the extension of financial market mechanisms to rural areas, and offers incentives to people to become entrepreneurs. It has also been pointed out that micro-credit initiatives often operate in a context of retrenchment of social services, and may be perceived as being offered for the purposes of avoiding public unrest (Gentil and Servet 2002: 760).

On the other hand, microcredit initiatives certainly share with human rights a focus on those marginalized by state and markets. Microcredit programmes tend to target the very poor, and, since poverty has a predominantly female face, women in particular: 99.5 per cent of BRAC beneficiaries are women (Halder 2003: 45). Studies on the impact on poverty of the extension of microcredit in Bangladesh yield contradictory results (cf. Halder 2003 and Hoque 2004). The government of Bangladesh takes the view that the economic results have been modest, while the aggregate social effects appear to be higher.[9] The government also recognizes that while growing involvement in microcredit-based enterprises helps increasing control of women over income, it has not led to lower risks of domestic violence against women.[10] Malnutrition levels in Bangladesh still show a marked gender disparity. As the UN Special Rapporteur on the right to food has stated, 'Women eat last and they eat least', a situation he characterizes as another form of violence.[11] Research also shows that male relatives control significant portions of women's loans, as well as the income-generating activities in which they are invested (Parmar 2003: 462).

A closer look at the operation and the philosophy of the Grameen Bank, whose founding father Muhammad Yunus is credited with creating the instrument, may shed some light on these apparent discrepancies.[12] In Yunus's view, the Grameen Bank operates as a 'market-based social entrepreneur'. This type of entrepreneur competes in the marketplace with all other competitors, but is inspired by a set of social objectives. In fact, the social objective is the basic reason for the business. The Grameen Bank has earned a profit, but that is only a secondary objective. Cost recovery is important, though, because it legitimizes the bank as a player in the marketplace. Successful market-based social entrepreneurs can draw on the resources of the market. The more numerous the market-based social entrepreneurs become, the more influence they gain in the business community, and the easier the access to 'the trillions of dollars of market capitalization money, part of which will find [this] just the right kind of investment'.

The Grameen Bank gives a high priority to building social capital. Groups and centres are formed. Leadership skills are

Box 7.2 *Grameen Bank, the Sixteen Decisions*

We respect the four principles of the Grameen Bank – we are disciplined, united, and courageous and workers – and we apply them to all our lives.

We wish to give our families good living standards.

We will not live in dilapidated houses. We repair them and work to build new ones.

We cultivate vegetables the whole year round and sell the surplus.

During the season for planting, we pick out as many seedlings as possible.

We intend to have small families. We shall reduce our expenses to a minimum. We take care of our health.

We educate our children and see that they can earn enough money to finance their training.

We see to it that our children and homes are clean.

We build latrines and use them.

We only drink water drawn from a well. If not, we boil the water or we use alum.

We will not accept a marriage dowry for our son and we do not give one to our daughter at her marriage. Our centre is against this practice.

We cause harm to no one and we will not tolerate that anyone should do us harm.

To increase our income, we make important investments in common.

We are always ready to help each other. When someone is in difficulty, we all give a helping hand.

If we learn that discipline is not respected in a centre, we go along to help and restore order.

We are introducing physical culture in all centres. We take part in all social events.

developed through the annual election of group and centre leaders. The Grameen Bank encourages borrowers to adopt, known as the 'Sixteen Decisions', goals in social, educational and health areas (see Box 7.2).

Not everyone takes a kindly view of how Grameen Bank weekly public meetings encourage socially responsible behaviour. It has been argued that the meetings are based on a culture of discipline and of reproducing male predominance in the relationship between male bank staff and female borrowers (Parmar 2003: 472).

From a human rights perspective, the Sixteen Decisions are striking because they do not approach social justice in terms of rights, but in terms of duties. In fact, the one right that the Grameen Bank promotes as a human right on its website is the (otherwise unknown) right to credit!

Human rights and human duties are not incompatible. An extensive debate has occurred within the human rights community as to whether human rights instruments sufficiently recognize the need for individuals to act responsibly and in a just and conscientious manner towards others (International Council on Human Rights 1999). Some have argued that there is a need for a universal declaration of human responsibilities – so far to no avail. Others argue, perhaps more convincingly, that human duties are of particular importance in *non-Western* societies. The African Charter on Human and Peoples' Rights includes a chapter on duties. Mutua shows how these duties are potentially useful for the protection of human dignity in the current African political context. Because the post-colonial African state has failed to enhance social solidarity, duties are necessary to strengthen community ties and social cohesiveness, creating a shared fate and common destiny (Mutua 2002: 87). Human duties *vis-à-vis* the community thus complement the protection individual rights offer. Likewise, it could well be argued that in

the context of extreme poverty in which the Grameen Bank operates, socially responsible behaviour within the poor communities
is essential if these communities are to achieve an improvement
in their living conditions.

Duties, though, are not rights; the concepts are not inter-
changeable. Rights perform a different, important function.
Parmar implicitly recognizes the difference when she analyses
the Grameen Bank's discourse on the empowerment of women.
She criticizes microcredit programmes for assuming that the
empowerment of women will be achieved through pressure by
micro-finance institutions on women to meet and take joint
responsibility for loans. Empowerment, she argues, cannot be
imposed by other agents of development, but must be driven by
women themselves: 'Consequently, the role of development practitioners in feminist liberation must undoubtedly be supportive
rather than central to this process of social change; it must be to
facilitate women's capacity to tackle injustice in their own lives,
and to act as allies in their struggles' (Parmar 2003: 463).

The author finds that microcredit programmes use peer pressure as an instrument to achieve financial efficiency rather than
solidarity for more social justice. All weighty decisions regarding programme design and implementation are in the hands
of professional staff, not of the women themselves. In human
rights language: because women are not recognized as holders
of human rights in their relationship with the institutions' own
staff and with society at large, the microcredit scheme does not
assist them in standing up to discrimination, or in insisting on
accountability.

Interestingly, BRAC, another major microcredit institution
in Bangladesh, explicitly commits itself to human rights in its
mission statement.[13] At the same time, the organization uses a
duty-based system of 'Eighteen Promises'. BRAC 'firmly believes
and is actively involved in promoting human rights, dignity and

gender equity through poor people's social, economic, political and human capacity building'. As part of its activities, BRAC runs a human rights training course, aimed at enabling people to protect themselves from illegal, unfair or discriminatory practices, and a legal aid clinic financially assisting people with litigation. In 2003, the organization reportedly notified 684 incidences of violence against women, 345 of which were cases of acid burning.

Without thorough field research, it is clearly impossible to evaluate whether BRAC's commitment to human rights in reality allows women to tackle injustice and achieve the accountability of those responsible for discrimination. A former student, Simone Longo de Andrade, travelled to Bangladesh in 2003, after having completed a thesis on microcredit from a human rights perspective.[14] She attended meetings of both Grameen Bank and BRAC borrower groups. The BRAC women knew what human rights were, while the Grameen Bank group was not so sure. The groups also answered her questions. In Simone's words:

> The things heard from the women were sometimes truly extraordinary. The questions that they raised were the missing link to a conclusion. BRAC's members were not interested in knowing, as Grameen Bank members were, if the person standing there and questioning them was married, had children, had parents still alive or her reason for her short hair. In BRAC, they were curious about the position of women, the existence of equal rights of both men and women or the existence of polygamy in the country she comes from.

The evidence is anecdotal at best, but does suggest that creating an environment in which human rights language is used encourages political awareness.

When human rights are added to the world of microcredit, empowerment strategies – to which micro-finance institutions are at least nominally committed – require an analysis of the political context from which poverty arises. Poverty is not accidental; it often results from the failure of human rights duty holders to perform their obligations. Therefore, solutions to poverty do not simply depend on increasing the available resources, but also on an increased acknowledgement of the rights of the poor. It is essential that micro-finance institutions demonstrate this through their internal mode of operation. The institutions should treat borrowers as holders of human rights. Only if women are encouraged to see themselves not simply as duty holders *vis-à-vis* the bank and others in the community, but as holders of rights which they enjoy *vis-à-vis* their husbands, their government and other actors who influence their ability to provide a living for themselves, and only if they are assisted in standing up for their rights in these different relationships, is there any hope that they will gain control over their living conditions.

Privatization and GATS

Privatization essentially refers to transfer of *ownership* from the public sector to the private sector. A state company is privatized when all its assets are sold to a private operator.

Sometimes the term is used in a wider sense to denote the transfer of (management) *tasks* from the government to the private sector. In this wider sense, a water network is privatized when a private company takes over the running of the system, even if the infrastructure remains public property.

Tasks may also be shared by the public and the private actor, creating a public/private partnership. In the example of the water system, it may well be that the state retains responsibility for putting up the investment required to expand the water network (particularly if the infrastructure remains public property), even after a private operator has taken over management.

Human rights are concerned with privatization whenever a human right covers the service that is about to be privatized.

196

Examples include the privatization of prisons, social security and healthcare benefits, systems for providing utilities such as electricity, gas and water. The consequence of privatization is that the state – the primary duty holder under human rights law – retreats as the actor responsible for service delivery. Instead of the state running a prison, a private actor takes over whose responsibility under human rights law is much more tenuous, and whose main motivation is the pursuit of private gain, not public responsibility.

Privatization does not necessarily have an adverse impact on human rights. Pre-privatization conditions, including the performance of the public provider, matter. Public companies may perform dismally in human rights terms. In any case, specific regulatory action is required to address the risk of human rights protection suffering as a consequence of the retreat of the state from service delivery. Practice demonstrates that, in the absence of such regulatory action, the privatization of a human-rights-sensitive service very often leads to violations of the human rights of users who are of no commercial interest to the private actor.

Interestingly, competition law, i.e. the law that promotes competition as an economic strategy, acknowledges that, for some services, providers are under a duty to take into account public interest requirements. In 2003, the European Commission produced a Green Paper on services of general interest that draws together common elements from existing sector-specific community law in order to establish a community concept of *universal service*:

> The concept of universal services refers to a set of general interest requirements ensuring that certain services are made available at a specified quality to all consumers and users throughout the territory of a Member State, independently of geographical location, and, in the light of specific national conditions, at an

affordable price. It has been developed specifically for some of the network industries (e.g. telecommunications, electricity, and postal services). The concept establishes the right for every citizen to access certain services considered as essential and imposes obligations on industries to provide a defined service at specified conditions, including complete territorial coverage. In a liberalized market environment, a universal service obligation guarantees that everybody has access at an affordable price and that the service quality is maintained, and, where necessary, improved.[15]

No link is established between the concept of 'universal service' and the human rights obligations of European states. According to the Commission paper, member-states are in principle free to define what they consider to be a universal service. Since there is no reference to human rights obligations, there is no guarantee that all services coming under the human rights regime will be recognized as 'universal' services. Under community competition law, the general interest obligations for service providers apply only if the service is a universal service. The obligations include obligations to ensure continuity, to maintain and develop the quality of the service, to offer the service at an affordable price in order to be accessible for everybody, and to provide for user and consumer protection. As explained below, such obligations are essential from a human rights perspective as well. The problem is that, in practice, the protection may not be available for human-rights-related services unless the relevant member-state accords the service the status of universal service. Clearly, this decision should not be a discretionary one if the provision of the service is covered by a state obligation under human rights law.

The failure to acknowledge the relevance of human rights obligations in international or domestic rules on privatization is not unique to Europe. Economic globalization creates an international climate that encourages states to engage in privatization (by providing a wide range of incentives for privatization, such as debt relief, or development assistance),[16] without a simultaneous insistence on the need to secure human rights during the process.

If the state is dependent on international assistance, privatization may well lead to a diminished ability to guarantee human rights, because the international institutions promoting privatization fail to take into account the effect on human rights of the measures they promote. The International Monetary Fund, for instance, whose financial support for addressing the balance of payment problems of developing countries is offered on condition that the state engages in privatization of public services, does not engage in an appraisal of the likely human rights impact, nor does it encourage measures to counteract any anticipated human rights violations (Darrow 2003: 277–8).

The General Agreement on Trade in Services (GATS) offers another example, developed here at more length.

Trade in services is not limited to cross-border supply. It also extends to 'commercial presence', which involves the supply of a service by one member through its commercial presence in the territory of another member. The agreement covers trade in services in twelve sectors, including many which are human-rights-sensitive, such as telecommunications, education, healthcare, environment and energy. The agreement excludes services supplied 'in the exercise of government authority' (Article I, 3, b, GATS). They are defined as services which are supplied neither on a 'commercial basis nor in competition with one or more service suppliers'. The exact scope of the provision is up for debate. If charging a fee is considered commercial, and the coexistence of public and private actors is considered as competition, few governmental services remain exempt (Chanda 2003: 2004).

GATS aims to liberalize the trade in services. Liberalization implies the opening up of (often previously monopolized) economic sectors to competition. In many developing and transition countries, governments were or are heavily involved in the provision of social services or utilities. In those cases, liberalization includes privatization, as state companies are sold to the highest bidder, or management of utilities is transferred to the private sector. The risk of a negative impact on human rights is real. The UN Special Rapporteur on the Right to Food has, for instance, found that recent examples of the privatization of water services have resulted in the increased exclusion of vulnerable groups, and a lack of accountability among private operators.[17]

The GATS system consists of two parts: the general rules and principles, and the commitments that states make in specific sectors. The general rules include the principle of non-discrimination known as 'most favoured nation' treatment; the promotion of transparency in relation to laws and regulations affecting trade in services; assurances that these regulations are applied in a reasonable, objective and impartial manner; a commitment to negotiate on the 'disciplining' use of public subsidies and government procurement, and, also, exceptions to the application of GATS in order to protect public morals, as well as human, animal and plant life.

In addition, GATS members make commitments on market access and national treatment in specific sectors. Commitments on market access set out the terms, limitations and conditions for market access, which a country must apply without discrimination to the services and service suppliers of all WTO members. A full commitment prohibits a country from limiting access to its services markets. Commitments on national treatment set out the conditions and qualifications on national services and service supply in a particular country, which will be applicable on a non-discriminatory basis to the services and service suppliers of other WTO members. A full commitment to 'national treatment' prohibits a state from discriminating between domestic and foreign 'like' services and service suppliers.

Commitments are voluntary. Countries decide freely what services they wish to open up, and what limitations they wish to maintain on market access and national treatment. The agreement, however, does bind members to successive rounds of negotiations, with a view to achieving a progressively higher level of liberalization. Once made, commitments can be modified or withdrawn after three years, but only if compensatory adjustment is offered.

Negotiations on commitments start with states tabling initial requests to other countries to open markets in specific sectors. This is followed by initial offers on the extent to which states are prepared to open their own market. Negotiations occur both bilaterally and multilaterally. The current round of largely confidential negotiations was opened in 2000.

The EU positions on both requests and offers were leaked on the internet.[18] The documents show a striking asymmetry between the EU's pressure on developing countries to open up services in markets such as water or energy, while at the same time not offering to liberalize the same services in Europe, ostensibly because it is concerned for the social impact of liberalization.

Technically, the GATS system as outlined above leaves intact the capacity of the state to take into account its human rights obligations in deciding whether or not to extend market access for human-rights-sensitive services, and under what conditions to do so. But GATS provides no incentives for taking human rights seriously. The system is not geared towards the provision of universal services, let alone towards the protection of human rights, but to progressive liberalization as such. GATS hands out rewards for opening markets to providers, but offers no prize for ensuring universal accessibility. The regime promotes opening up health services to foreign operators regardless of whether costs to users rise, but discourages the provision of subsidies to ensure access to all of primary healthcare. Similarly to the TRIPs agreement, GATS operates as a self-contained system geared towards achieving trade objectives only, pushing those governments arguing human rights obligations into a defensive position.

From a human rights perspective, it is essential that GATS negotiators: (i) delay opening markets in human-rights-sensitive services to private foreign operators until they have ensured that the domestic legal system provides the *specific* human rights protection (see below) necessary to prevent and redress the potential adverse human rights impacts of the liberalization/ privatization process; and (ii) ensure that GATS commitments are drafted in such a way that the state preserves the necessary regulatory capability to comply with its human rights duties after the relevant service has been brought under the GATS scheme.

Will the GATS negotiators hear the message? Few have human rights expertise. Even developed countries have great difficulty in mainstreaming human rights. National parliaments play a limited role during negotiations, and are not heard until the end of the process when the executive seeks ratification of the internationally agreed text. GATS negotiations occur beyond the purview of domestic democratic institutions. As Darrow argues, discussions on human-rights-sensitive services were once local, within the sphere of public participation and public accountability, but have now become international, 'far removed from the influence of the governed' (Darrow 2003: 105).

This removal of the issues from the political realm makes it crucial for international human rights NGOs to invest in WTO debates. If decision-making on human-rights-sensitive services moves from the domestic to the global level, then so must the action of human rights organizations. Clearly, human rights organizations cannot substitute for parliaments but, in the current stage of global governance, there may be few other ways of ensuring at least some degree of downward accountability.

This still leaves the question of what specific mechanisms are required at the domestic level to ensure continued human rights protection in a context of privatization. Ratification of international human rights treaties clearly does not suffice, because the treaties do not offer specifics on the consequences of the transfer of responsibility to a private actor of a service covered by a treaty right.

The starting point is crystal clear. The state cannot absolve itself of human rights responsibility by contracting out service provision to private bodies or individuals. The state remains responsible under human rights treaties even after the privatization of the service has occurred. What changes is the type of duty. After privatization, the state needs to provide protection for individuals against abuses by the private actor, instead of simply respecting the duty itself. The state will be able to provide protection only if it creates mechanisms for overseeing the human rights impact of service delivery by the private actor, and for intervening when the situation takes a bad turn. The need for such specific instruments emerges only in the context of privatization. In short: privatization requires an adjustment of state human rights duties to the new context.

There may well be a need to go further, to look beyond the horizon of state obligations. Clearly, the establishment of the human rights duties of the private operator would provide an important additional safeguard. Such human rights duties can easily be constructed. Privatization contracts covering human rights services inevitably involve the private operator in actions that touch the public interest. The contracts become an essential instrument for the development and realization of human rights. The private operator can decide freely whether or not he wishes to enter into such a contract, but if he does, his role in society changes; he is no longer a purely private actor, but an operator delivering a service of general interest. The relevant human rights come within the company's sphere of influence and, thus, as the UN sub-commission has suggested, the company should be considered as a duty holder under human rights law.

Ideally, domestic legislation and the privatization contract should confirm the existence of corporate human rights duties in these circumstances. The South African Constitution, for example, 'binds a natural or a juristic person if, and to the extent that, it is applicable, taking into account the nature of the right and the nature of any duty imposed by the right'.

What legal techniques are at the disposal of the state to ensure human rights protection during privatization? In England and Wales, legislation provides for the coexistence of a system of competitive private ownership of the electricity industry within the overarching competence of the Secretary of State for Energy and a regulatory authority to ensure competition, but also to protect the interests of consumers and the environment. Birdsall and Nellis point out that the creation of an independent, accountable regulatory regime ensures a much better distributional outcome from privatization: 'Selling governments and those that assist them, should invest more upfront attention and effort in the creation and strengthening of regulatory capacity, and less in organizing quick transactions' (Birdsall and Nellis 2003: 1628).

In England and Wales, the regulatory authority and the Secretary of State are required by law to take into account factors such as the need to satisfy all reasonable demands for power and to take into account the special interests of disabled or chronically sick persons, pensioners and rural dwellers – vulnerable groups in human rights terms. Provision is made for consumer views, and detailed standards have been set for private operators *vis-à-vis* consumers (including on diffusion of information) that are enforceable by fines (Botchway 2000: 819–23). The creation of a legal relationship between the user and the private operator is important, because such a relationship does not automatically exist. Privatization contracts are concluded between the state and the private operator. Users may not be able to rely on a contract to which they are not a party.

The length of the contract is relevant as well. Shorter contracts make it easier for the state to insist on compliance when the performance of the service falls below human rights standards. Long-term contracts allow much more leeway to the private operator (e.g. in deciding on long-term price levels). Long-term contracts with a clause allowing renegotiation at specified intervals may offer a compromise between the private actor's interest in securing a return for a potentially expensive investment, and the state's interest in ensuring affordable access.

The state should make a commitment to the users of the service on the maintenance of performance standards at a level required by its human rights obligations. This commitment then creates a legitimate expectation on the part of the consumer, who, in case of non-performance, can bring a complaint against the state under administrative law. The organization of regular public hearings both during the privatization process and during the actual operation of the privatized regime may also be a useful device for ensuring that human rights concerns are taken into account.

The reality of privatization may, however, be far removed from such an ideal script. Consider the broadly reported privatization of the water system of Bolivia's third largest city, Cochabamba.

The privatization of the water system in Cochabamba was part of a larger privatization process that started in Bolivia in the mid-1980s. The World Bank supported the process. The municipal company that provided water before privatization had incurred significant debts, which were pardoned by the Bank on the condition that privatization would occur. In 1999, following a process with a single bidder, a forty-year concession was granted to Aguas del Tunari, a majority-owned subsidiary of the US company Bechtel. A state monopoly was thus replaced by a private monopoly. Within weeks of taking over the management of the water system, the company raised water rates significantly. The increase in price led to massive demonstrations which the government attempted to suppress, including by the use of violence. Civil society pressure was such, however, that in April 2000 the government announced the cancelling of the contract with Aguas del Tunari, and returned the management of the water service to the municipal company. It would have been much more difficult for the government to take this decision if Bolivia had already committed itself under GATS to liberalize water services. The civil society coordinating committee that had campaigned against the privatization now became a partner in the management of the municipal company.

Aguas del Tunari left Bolivia and moved its corporate headquarters to the Netherlands, in order to make use of a bilateral investment treaty between the Netherlands and Bolivia that creates jurisdiction for the International Centre for the Settlement of Investment Disputes (ICSID) to hear cases between Dutch companies and Bolivia. Through this legal action the investor hopes to recover losses incurred.

ICSID was a 1965 World Bank initiative. The Bank still meets the full cost of the ICSID secretariat, and there are 'close ties' (Shihata 1991: 292) between both institutions. Cases are usually heard by three arbitrators 'of high moral character and recognized competence in the fields of law, commerce, industry or finance, who may be relied upon to exercise independent judgment'. The proceedings are confidential. All the ICSID secretariat does is publish a list of pending cases. The tribunal decides a dispute in accordance with the law agreed by the parties. In the absence of such an agreement, the arbiters apply the domestic law of the state party to the dispute (including its rules on the conflict of laws) and such rules of international law as may be applicable. In any case, the dispute will 'effectively be internationalised in that the ultimate standard of decision will be provided by international law' (Muchlinski 1999: 551). Awards are binding on the parties and not subject to appeal. States are under an obligation to ensure enforcement of an award in the domestic legal system. The Aguas del Tunari case is still pending. The tribunal held hearings on its jurisdiction in February 2004 in Washington.

The Aguas del Tunari story perfectly illustrates the concerns raised above. The events in Bolivia underscore the importance of grassroots mobilization and political action to counter a privatization process with an adverse impact on human rights. It is equally significant, however, that the dispute has now moved to an essentially private arbitration system that does not provide a role for the social movements that were at the basis of the government's decision to annul the contract. The ICSID procedure takes the privatization exercise out of the public realm, out of Bolivia, and back to Washington, the headquarters of the World Bank where the story started. Recently, the Bolivian social movements who had appealed to the ICSID tribunal to be allowed to participate actively in the proceedings were informed by the president of the tribunal arbitrating the dispute, that the tribunal had no power to open the proceedings to the public or to provide access to documents filed in the dispute without the consent of the parties. This may well be the law under the ICSID convention, but it offers further evidence of the blindfolds worn by international economic dispute settlement systems. These institutions are simply not equipped to deal properly with disputes on privatization that have serious human rights consequences.

If the ICSID tribunal finds that it has jurisdiction – this may not be obvious (cf. Muchlinski 1999: 558) – it will be of great interest to see how it engages with a human-rights-based defence. The UN High Commissioner for Human Rights has taken a position on the Aguas del Tunari events: 'The reversal of the decision to liberalize water services is consistent, under the circumstances, with the Government's obligation to ensure access to an adequate supply of safe drinking water as a component of the right to health.'[19]

Under the ICSID convention, the tribunal is not barred from considering human rights law as part of the law applicable to the dispute. In fact, the tribunal has a wonderful opportunity to recognize the primacy of human rights and demonstrate concern for those marginalized by both the government and the private operator. Similar disputes involving privatization schemes in Argentina also require the taking into account of the human rights impact of the tribunal's decisions. But, given the setting to which the tribunal belongs, it is much more likely that the outcome will be driven by a concern to establish secure conditions for international investment.

In conclusion, in theory states are able to maintain human rights protection during a privatization process and afterwards, *if* specific regulation aimed at ensuring human rights protection is in place. Often such regulation will imply a shift of part of the cost to provide for the human-rights-sensitive services to the private investor (if only by limiting his profits) in order to ensure the continuity of the provision of the service to marginalized groups in society unable to pay the commercial price.

Whether economic realities will permit least developed countries in particular to find a private company that is interested in operating under conditions compatible with human rights protection is far from certain. In his comparative study of privatizations of electricity systems, Botchway (2000: 814–18) finds that in the one least developed country included in the survey – the Côte d'Ivoire – privatization of the electricity sector occurred without social protection, under a prime minister who was a former IMF technocrat.

If specific human rights protection is not in place, privatization of human-rights-related services should not be undertaken.

Agrarian reform

Unequal distribution of land causes rural poverty. Agrarian reform as traditionally defined seeks to transfer control and ownership of agricultural land to the actual tillers. Transfer of ownership is effective only if the new owners are provided with support services, such as physical infrastructure (irrigation, roads), economic services (access to credit) and social support (building farmers' organizations, providing training). The land targeted for redistribution may be public (e.g. the transfer of state-owned assets to individuals in transition countries) or private (e.g. because the ownership structure of land is extremely unequal or because landowners fail to exploit potentially productive land). The new owners may hold the land individually or enjoy a form of communal property.

Agrarian reform depends on a strong state driven by social justice concerns. State involvement as such is not enough. Fantu Cheru notes that, in Africa, states have traditionally played a central role in the production and marketing of agriculture, but 'to the detriment of the very subsistence farmers whom they claim to protect and support' (Cheru 2002: 94). A wide divide separates elite bureaucrats and party loyalists from the reality of rural life. Prices paid to farmers are kept artificially low, providing cheap food for the urban population, while taxation on agricultural production is high. Marketing boards, which are at the centre of this process, are 'symbols of oppression' (ibid., p. 95).

Rural women, in particular, are invisible to domestic policy-makers, partly because of traditional values and restrictions on access for women to productive resources under customary law;

209

but even when the state becomes involved with determining how land should be used, the result may well exclude access to land for women, because 'women suffer systematic disadvantages both in the market and in state-backed systems of property ownership, either because their opportunities to buy land are very limited, or because local-level authorities practise gender discrimination, preventing women from claiming rights that are in theory backed by law' (Whitehead and Tsikata 2003: 79). Change requires 'an aggressive government policy to remove the legal obstacles to women's equal participation in the rural economy' (Cheru 2002: 108).

State involvement does not, as such, guarantee prioritization of landless farmers, farm workers or subsistence farmers. Nor does the international context necessarily facilitate land poli-cies driven by social justice concerns. Policy prescriptions to developing countries focus on the production of cash crops for export (which includes a bias in favour of large-scale intensive farming), the liberalization of agricultural imports (including of crops required for basic needs satisfaction, to be provided by the TNCs that dominate the global trade in agriculture) and the cutting of subsidies for agricultural producers. Such prescrip-tions encourage governments to direct their efforts towards making land available for export plantations rather than to small farmers. Public infrastructure support also targets export produc-tion. The needs of small farmers receive less attention.

The World Bank promotes a market-assisted approach to agrarian reform:

> Market assisted land reform programs differ from government directed land reform primarily in the institutional mechanisms used to transfer land. In a market assisted land reform, benefici-aries receive a combination of grants and loans from the public and private sectors which they use to negotiate the purchase of

land from willing sellers. The willing seller–willing buyer framework of market assisted land reform contrasts with government directed land reform in which the government dispossess the land from a large farm and give it free of charge to the poor. At the same time it lowers the cost of the land reform programs, it increases the incentives for beneficiaries to make productive use of their lands. Market assisted land reform thus can avoid the problems of bloated bureaucracies and non-working farms seen in some past land reform programs.

In an ideal scenario, farmers are able to repay the loan with the income the land yields. Whether the ideal scenario happens not only depends on the farmer's individual capital and skills, but also on the quality of the land that the landowner is willing to sell, and on domestic and international support policies for small-scale farming. As Borras (1999: 5) points out, market-assisted land policies are not driven by social justice, but by concerns about economic efficiency.

The social consequences of unequal distribution of land will inevitably need to be tackled at the three different levels of society, state and international community. As Cheru (2000: 58) argues, rural peoples should be able to organize themselves at the community level. Local-level organizations should be given greater control over the allocation of resources, and over the officials that serve them. Agrarian reform also requires pro-reform initiatives 'from above', i.e. initiatives by actors within the state that are supportive, or at least tolerant of social mobilization from below (Borras 1999: 7). Finally, international efforts, both intergovernmental and non-governmental, should support such domestic alliances if they are to stand any chance of surviving in a market-based global economy. What is needed is not simply coexistence, but cooperation between the three levels. Can a human rights approach help?

Article 11 of the International Covenant on Economic, Social and Cultural Rights, on the right to food, requires states to take measures to improve methods of production, conservation and distribution of food including 'by developing or reforming agrarian systems in such a ways as to achieve the most effective development and utilization of natural resources'. Astonishingly, the UN Committee on ESC Rights ignored the paragraph in its general comment on the right to food.[20] The general comment defines the core content of the right to adequate food in terms of availability and accessibility. Food should be available 'in a quantity and quality sufficient to satisfy the dietary needs of individuals, free from adverse substances, and acceptable within a given culture'. The document recognizes that socially vulnerable groups 'such as landless people' may need attention through special programmes, and that discrimination in access to food needs to be prevented, including 'by providing guarantees of full and equal access to economic resources, particularly for women, including the right to inheritance and the ownership of land and other property'.

In November 2004, the Council of the Food and Agricultural Organization adopted voluntary guidelines on the right to food that includes the following cautious provision on agrarian reform:

States should take measures to promote and protect the security of land tenure, especially with respect to women, poor and disadvantaged segments of society, through legislation that protects the full and equal right to own land and other property, including the right to inherit. As appropriate, states should consider establishing legal and other policy mechanisms, consistent with their international human rights obligations and in accordance with the rule of law, that advance land reform to enhance access for the poor and women. Such mechanisms should also promote conservation and sustainable use of land. Special consideration should be given to the situation of indigenous communities.[21]

The High Commissioner for Human Rights in 2002 produced a paper on the impact of the WTO Agreement on Agriculture on human rights. The paper confirms that a human rights approach to trade liberalization focuses on protecting vulnerable individuals and groups – in particular, low-income and resource-poor farmers, as well as farm labourers and rural communities. Leaving greater flexibility in the Agreement on Agriculture for developing countries to raise tariffs and grant domestic support for these farmers should have only minor trade-distorting effects and would positively affect their human rights. Similarly, the paper argues that food-insecure states should enjoy a higher limit for domestic support for basic foodstuffs compared to non-food crops or non-food-security crops.[22]

These documents represent no more than a modest contribution to the debate on agrarian reform. Land reform proponents may not be impressed. This is a shame because, potentially, human rights have more to offer to the issue of agrarian reform than is currently provided by the human rights institutions. No human rights approach can be relevant without an insight into the living conditions of small farmers. Such an insight can be gained from affected communities, and from agrarian reform activists working on their behalf. A human rights approach will work only if it understands the language used by land reform proponents, and identifies a common agenda round which alliances can be forged. The challenge is not limited to teaching land reform proponents about what constitutes the right to food – human rights activists always undertake such a task with great enthusiasm – it also includes rethinking human rights in order to enhance their relevance to the problem at hand. It is a two-way process. On an issue such as land reform, alliances are essential because the market approach is dominant. That approach does not have a major interest in the group on which both land reform proponents and human rights activists focus. In a context where the dominant discourse is antagonistic, alliances are a necessity not simply a choice.

At Maastricht University, in 2002, we brought together a group of representatives of farmers, development and human rights organizations and academia to discuss the issue of agrarian reform and human rights. The working conference was a joint initiative of the centre for human rights at the university and three NGOs: Via Campesina, FIAN and 11.11.11. At the end of the seminar, a concluding document was adopted, later published by FIAN.[23]

The concluding document is not particularly important from a political point of view, but it is conceptually of interest. It resulted from three days of dialogue between human rights and land reform proponents, and constituted an attempt to bridge conceptual gaps. This was not an easy exercise. The participants identified a common concern: 'that land is not a mere commodity, but the basis of a justified and dignified livelihood for many rural communities the world over'. The legal basis for the expression of this concern came from a variety of human rights sources. The key paragraph from the document reads: 'Therefore, we: Promote the right of just, equitable and ecologically sustainable access to productive resources, integrating the right to livelihood, to housing and food. We reaffirm that this right implies obligations, derived from all legal frameworks, whether customary, common, civil, religious or indigenous, in so far as these promote the just and equitable access to productive resources.'

The 'right of access to productive resources' is a right that does not appear in international human rights conventions. 'Access to productive resources' is a formula used by proponents of agrarian reform. The contribution of the human rights community was to articulate the concern in the language of rights (and thus they insisted that relevant actors had a duty to engage in land reform under certain circumstances, and that mechanisms must be available to hold them accountable in the case of failure to perform) but also to link the notion of access to productive resources with widely recognized human rights to adequate living, housing and food. The formula was intended to indicate that a bundle of existing rights could be used in an integrated way to support the claim to access to productive resources. Whether the formula will ever receive recognition in a legal document is uncertain, but this is perhaps not the point. The real test is whether the text makes sense as a 'text of resistance' (in Rajagopal's phrase), and whether the document can contribute to an improved understanding, and as a basis for common action, between agrarian reform and human rights proponents.

Another lesson confirmed by the exercise was that human rights law can offer effective protection only if it operates at all relevant levels: at the level of the international community, the state and society. Land reform proponents more naturally address the three levels by simply looking at impact; human rights activists are constrained by the state orientation inherent in human rights treaty law. The concluding document recognized that not only states hold obligations, but also private (transnational) actors and international organizations. The text included a special focus on the World Bank, and stated that the concept of voluntary land distribution did not reflect the obligation to use the maximum of available resources to fulfil the right to food.

The dialogue between human rights and land reform proponents also resulted in an increased emphasis on the role of societal mechanisms, such as customary law. The concluding document argued that local and national duty holders may not only have obligations arising from international law, but from customary law as well. Certainly, the issue was not fully resolved.

The text recognized that customary law could be empowering in many respects, but that its content and role also had to be reviewed critically, e.g. from a gender perspective.

In conclusion, on each of the issues discussed in this chapter, the human rights approach offers additional insights into how relevant policies should be shaped in order to improve the unacceptable living conditions of marginalized communities.

On the other hand, the experiences of marginalized communities must inform the human rights discourse. Reaching out to these communities requires a conscious effort to understand and accommodate the language they use when formulating claims. Their claims may well be human rights claims even if they are not phrased in human rights language.

Human rights proponents need proactively to identify the human rights impact of economic globalization, if human rights are to fulfil their potential as instruments of social protection. They need to do so at an early stage, when economic norms and mechanisms are being negotiated. Human rights concerns must be part and parcel of the regulation of economic globalization. If they are, the benefits from the perspective of the enforceability of human rights may well be impressive. Economic dispute settlement systems tend to provide much stronger incentives for compliance than the monitoring systems attached to human rights conventions. Integration of human rights concerns will therefore improve their enforceability.

Notes

1 Office of the High Commissioner for Human Rights, *5th WTO Ministerial Conference (10–14 September 2003), Human Rights and Trade*, 8.

2 UN Committee on ESC Rights, 'General Comment no. 14: The Right to the Highest Attainable Standard of Health (Article 12)', UN doc. E/C.12/2000/4 (11 August 2000), par. 12.

3 UN Committee on ESC Rights, 'Statement on Human Rights and Intellectual Property', UN doc. E/C.12/2001/15 (14 December 2001), par. 4.

4 UN Committee on ESC Rights, 'General Comment no. 14', par. 50.

5 UN Sub-Commission on the Promotion and Protection of Human Rights, Resolution 2000/7 (17 August 2000), pars 2–3. The resolution was adopted without a vote.

6 UN Committee on ESC Rights, 'Statement on Human Rights and Intellectual Property', UN doc. E/C.12/2001/15 (14 December 2001), par. 10.

7 UN Economic and Social Council, Resolution 1998/28 (29 July 1998).

8 Compare the Virtual Library on Microcredit compiled by the Global Development Research Centre at <www.gdrc.org>

9 Government of Bangladesh (2001), *Action Programme for the Development of Bangladesh (2001–2010)*, p. 23. Country presentation to the third UN Conference on the Least Developed Countries.

10 Ibid., 7.

11 The report on the Special Rapporteur's mission to Bangladesh was published as UN doc. E/CN.4/2004/10/Add. 1 (29 October 2003). See pars 7, 48.

12 The information that follows was collected from different sources on the Grameen Bank website at <www.grameen-info.org>

13 See the BRAC website at <www.brac.net>

14 The thesis is available on request from the European Master in Human Rights and Democratization at <www.eiuc.org>

15 Commission Green Paper on Services of General Interest, COM(2003), 270 final (21 May 2003), par. 50.

16 Compare Art. 21, Cotonou ACP–EU Partnership Agreement (23 June 2000).

17 See UN doc. E/CN.4/Sub.2/2002/59 (1 March 2002), pars 49–65.

18 See <www.gatswatch.org>

19 See UN doc. E/CN.4/Sub.2/2002/9 (25 June 2002), par. 49.

20 UN Committee on ESC Rights, 'General Comment no. 12: The Right to Adequate Food', UN doc. E/C.12/1999/5 (12 May 1999).

21 FAO Council, Voluntary Guidelines to support the progressive realization of the right to adequate food in the context of national food security (22–27 Novemeber 2004), Guideline 8b.

22 UN doc. E/CN.4/2002/54 (15 January 2002), in particular pars 47–8.

23 FIAN *Agrarian Reform and Human Rights. Seminar Report* (15–17 April 2002) (Heidelberg: FIAN, 2003).

8 | Conclusion

The human rights regime as it functions today can be easily criticized. The regime reflects the distribution of power in international relations. The distribution of power influences which norms become recognized as universal norms. It determines whether action against violations is undertaken. Limited tools are available to hold powerful states responsible when they commit human rights violations. Dominant economic actors promote a market-friendly approach to human rights that selects elements from the discourse favourable to their interests, and ignores others. There is nothing holy or immaculate about the world of human rights.

Nevertheless, the need for human rights protection is as urgent in the age of the market as it was at the time of the Cold War. The right of each and every person to live in human dignity needs to be reaffirmed, particularly when the market justifies exclusion of those who compete poorly. The exclusiveness of the market needs to be countered by the inclusiveness of human rights. Human rights have this potential, but only if they adjust to the challenges of economic globalization, and if they are supported by a sufficiently strong and broad alliance of forces within and among different societies.

The existing catalogue of civil, cultural, economic, political and social rights, as expressed in the international law of human rights, remains a valid point of departure. Doors should not be closed but be open to the recognition of multiple human rights duty holders; open to going beyond law in thinking about human rights; and open to connecting global norms and local realities.

This change, not in ideals but in attitude, is required because in the current era of economic globalization, and the internationalization of political violence that it entails, the need for protection has changed. It may well change again in the future. Human rights have to be a living instrument in order to deliver on the promise of protection they hold.

Economic globalization requires the recognition of multiple human rights duty holders. Human rights are no longer affected only by the state, which has territorial control over the area where people live. Decisions by intergovernmental organizations, by economic or violent non-state actors and by other states have far-reaching consequences for the degree to which human rights are enjoyed in a particular part of the world. None of these other actors is, however, sufficiently accountable for the human rights impact of their actions *vis-à-vis* people affected by their activities.

The vision is of a web of human rights obligations, with the territorially responsible country still at the centre but no longer alone. No trade-off need occur between holding the state responsible for human rights violations and simultaneously developing the human rights responsibilities of other actors.

Perhaps the clearest examples are in the field of corporate responsibility for human rights. When companies have a direct impact on the quality of life of entire communities, because they exploit the land off which people live or because they provide a service essential to survival needs, effective human rights protection requires downwards accountability both by the state when it fails to prevent abuses by the private actor, and by the private actor directly when it commits abuses falling within its sphere of influence.

Similarly, an adequate response to the adverse human rights impact of IMF-sponsored economic reforms requires not only investigation of the human rights responsibility of the International

Monetary Fund as an international organization, but also of the responsibilities of the state that agrees to the measures and those that supplied the required majority within the institution.

In a context of globalization, human rights protection cannot be ensured unless multiple actors (are made to) accept responsibility for human rights. This finding applies across the whole range of economic, social and cultural rights, and of civil and political rights. An appropriate human rights response to terrorist attacks by non-state actors that organize across borders equally depends on establishing accountability for multiple actors.

That human rights are legal rights is important, because law is important for the purposes of providing protection. Reparation for violations of human rights is easier to achieve for victims if the law obliges the duty bearer to repair the damage. Dependency on a political process only offers fewer guarantees of a human-rights-friendly outcome.

Law is also important because of its general applicability. In principle, the law applies even if its application in specific circumstances is politically awkward or detrimental to dominant interests. Torture is no less prohibited legally because it is committed by an industrialized state, or because emotions run high in a society that was the target of a terrorist attack. Law can be a powerful tool to protect the dignity of all human life. The attitude of domestic and international judges – their willingness to insist on respect for the letter of what was laid down and to find against perpetrators of human rights violations – is essential in providing human rights protection. The 'ideal' scenario happens when a credible accountability mechanism can deal with the human rights responsibilities of all relevant actors under a system of law that recognizes the primacy of human rights. In short: the legal recognition of human rights is something well worth fighting for.

On the other hand, the law on the books is often deficient

because the international or domestic legislator does not stand apart from the power relations discussed above. Human rights law may well be far removed from the reality of local human rights struggles. In response, it is important that civil society asserts normative prerogatives of its own in the human rights field – that it claims ownership of human rights on behalf of those facing repression. Texts of resistance offer a welcome contrast to official sources of human rights law.

In addition, legal mechanisms are not the only instruments through which human rights protection can be provided. The invocation of human rights may well permit the opening of political space for the voices of marginalized communities, even if their claims are not recognized before a court of law. The World Bank Inspection Panel procedure primarily serves this purpose. The procedure renders groups visible that both the borrower and the Bank were happy to ignore. Political processes are no less important for the realization of human rights than legislation.

Framing claims in terms of human rights also allows local communities to connect to the international human rights movement. Using the language of human rights facilitates the identification of common problems and solutions, and permits making use of resources that the international human rights movement can contribute to the domestic struggle. These resources may well include the capacity to mobilize international public opinion on behalf of the community's plight. In situations that implicate multiple domestic and foreign actors in human rights violations, the involvement of the international human rights movement may well be a necessity, and not simply a matter of choice.

Human rights are also instruments of grassroots mobilization *within* the relevant communities. The language of rights suggests that the living conditions the community finds itself in are not simply unfortunate, but fundamentally unjust. Strength and self-confidence can be derived from that starting point, even if enforceability of human rights at the domestic level is difficult. The societal value of human rights is not limited to their legal value. Consequently, the legal discipline should not be the only one that evaluates the usefulness of human rights or decides their future development.

Finally, care should be taken that human rights do not become one more instrument of homogenization. The risk exists because human rights are, at least in part, global norms that seek to offer protection to every individual.

There does not have to be a contradiction between establishing global rules and giving specific meaning to those rules on the basis of the living experiences of those facing abuse. Living experiences inevitably vary enormously across the globe. The activities of transnational companies may, for example, have very different impacts on human rights in different societies, and the specific techniques needed to offer protection to different communities will vary accordingly. On the other hand, it makes eminent sense equally to define the human rights responsibilities of transnational companies at the global level, precisely because they act globally. The same reasoning applies when a human rights response needs to be developed to deal with the adverse impact of WTO rules or of decisions of the international financial institutions. If some of the causes of human rights violations are global, the response needs to be global as well.

No conceptual obstacles prevent the accommodation of plurality within the human rights regime. What accommodating plurality does require is an insight into how contestations over rights take place at the local level, and a concern for the practical circumstances which determine whether at that level protection will be real. The human rights response will need to be localized in order to be effective, and in that sense will have to be superior over strategies of economic globalization that offer a single global recipe. The different approaches taken by the inter-American and African human rights protection systems to disputes over land accompanied by major violations of human rights are not a threat to the universality of human rights, but a strength. They demonstrate that the common language of human rights is sufficiently flexible to incorporate the different ways in which communities and governments analyse a problem, i.e. in the cases at hand in terms of indigenous concepts of property or in terms of collective rights of peoples.

Human rights need to be informed by an analysis of how globalization operates, and adapt to the challenge. The move towards multiplicity of human rights duty holders becomes much more self-evident if human rights proponents learn from development practitioners. Lawyers need to interact with social scientists in order to understand the conditions which determine whether or not human rights protection is effective. Those interested in universal human rights and global institutions need to go into the field and witness human rights struggles at the local level. From this dialogue, a much enriched concept of human rights will emerge that can fulfil the promise of securing social justice in the age of the market.

References

Abdullah, H. (2000) *Economic, Social and Cultural Rights in Nigeria* (Stockholm: Swedish NGO Foundation for Human Rights).

Agbakwa, S. (2002) 'Reclaiming Humanity: Economic, Social and Cultural Rights as the Cornerstone of African Human Rights', *Yale Human Rights and Development Law Journal*, vol. 5: 177–216.

Alston, P. and J. Crawford (eds) (2000) *The Future of Human Rights Treaty Monitoring* (Cambridge: Cambridge University Press).

Aman, A. (2000) 'Administrative Law for a New Century', in A. Prakash and J. Hart (eds), *Globalization and Governance* (London: Routledge), pp. 267–88.

Amnesty International (2004) *The UN Human Rights Norms for Business: Towards Legal Accountability* (London: Amnesty International).

Anderson, K. (2002) 'Microcredit: Fulfilling or Belying the Universalist Morality of Globalizing Markets?', *Yale Human Rights and Development Law Journal*, vol. 5: 85–122.

Appadurai, A. (1999) 'Disjuncture and Difference in the Global Cultural Economy', in S. During (ed.), *The Cultural Studies Reader* (London: Routledge), pp. 220–30.

Athreya, B. (2002) 'Women in the Global Economy', in V. Desai and R. Potter (eds), *The Companion to Development Studies* (London: Arnold), pp. 342–6.

Baxi, U. (2002) *The Future of Human Rights* (New Delhi: Oxford University Press).

Bekker, G. (2003) 'The Social and Economic Rights Action Center and the Center for Economic and Social Rights/Nigeria', *Journal of African Law*, vol. 47, no. 1: 126–32.

Bello, W. (2002) *Deglobalization* (London: Zed Books).

Bhaduri, A. (2002) 'Nationalism and Economic Policy', in D. Nayyar (ed.), *Governing Globalization* (Oxford: Oxford University Press), pp. 19–48.

Bhagwati, J. (2003) 'Borders Beyond Control', *Foreign Affairs*, vol. 82, no. 1: 98–104.

Birdsall, N. and J. Nellis (2003) 'Winners and Losers: Assessing Distributional Impact of Privatisation', *World Development*, vol. 31: 1617–33.

Björkman, H. (ed.) (1999) *Human Development and Human Rights*.

Report of the Oslo Symposium (Oslo: UNDP, UN Office of the High Commissioner for Human Rights/Royal Ministry of Norway).

Borras, S. (1999) *The Bibingka Strategy in Land Reform Implementation* (Quezon City: Institute for Popular Democracy).

Botchway, F. (2000) 'The Role of the State in the Context of Good Governance and Electricity Management: Comparative Antecedents and the Current Trends', *University of Pennsylvania Journal of International Economic Law*, vol. 21: 781–832.

Brysk, A. (ed.) (2002) *Globalization and Human Rights* (Berkeley: University of California Press).

Cesari, J. (2002) 'Global Multiculturalism: The Challenge of Heterogeneity', *Alternatives*, vol. 27: 5–19.

Chanda, R. (2003) 'Social Services and the GATS: Key Issues and Concerns', *World Development*, vol. 31: 1997–2011.

Chapman, A. (2002) 'Core Obligations Related to ICESCR Article 15(1)(c)', in A. Chapman and S. Russell (eds), *Core Obligations: Building a Framework for Economic, Social and Cultural Rights* (Antwerp: Intersentia), pp. 305–31.

Chapman, A. and S. Russell (2002) 'Introduction', in A. Chapman and S. Russell (eds), *Core Obligations: Building a Framework for Economic, Social and Cultural Rights* (Antwerp: Intersentia), pp. 1–19.

Cheru, F. (2002) *African Renaissance* (London: Zed Books).

Clapham, A. and S. Jerbi (2001) 'Categories of Corporate Complicity in Human Rights Abuses', *Hastings International and Comparative Law*, vol. 24: 339–50.

Clifford, B. (2002) 'Globalization and the Social Construction of Human Rights Campaigns', in A. Brysk (ed.), *Globalization and Human Rights* (Berkeley: University of California Press), pp. 133–47.

COHRE (Centre on Housing Rights and Forced Evictions) (2003) *Litigating Economic, Social and Cultural Rights: Achievements, Challenges and Strategies* (Geneva: COHRE).

Coomans, F. (2003) 'The *Ogoni* Case Before the African Commission on Human and Peoples' Rights', *International and Comparative Law Quarterly*, vol. 52: 749–60.

Coomans, F. and M. Kamminga (eds) (2004) *Extraterritorial Application of Human Rights Treaties* (Antwerp: Intersentia).

Cortázar, J. (1983), 'Avant-propos' in E. Jouve (ed.), *Un tribunal pour les peuples* (Paris: Berger-Levrault), pp. 7–12.

Darrow, M. (2003) *Between Light and Shadow. The World Bank, the International Monetary Fund and International Human Rights Law* (Oxford: Hart Publishing).

Deere, C. (2003) 'Women's Land Rights and Rural Social Movements in the Brazilian Agrarian Reform', in S. Razavi (ed.), *Agrarian Change, Gender and Land Rights* (Oxford: Blackwell), pp. 257–88.

De Feyter, K. (2001a) *World Development Law* (Antwerp: Intersentia).

— (2001b) 'Corporate Governance and Human Rights', in Institut International des Droits de L'Homme (ed.), *Commerce mondial et protection des droits de l'homme* (Brussels: Bruylant), pp. 71–110.

Desai, V. and R. Potter (eds) (2002) *The Companion to Development Studies* (London: Arnold).

DFID (2000) *Human Rights for Poor People* (London: DFID [Department for International Development] UK).

Dugard, J. (2000) 'The Role of Human Rights Treaty Standards in Domestic Law: The South African Experience', in P. Alston and J. Crawford (eds), *The Future of Human Rights Treaty Monitoring* (Cambridge: Cambridge University Press), pp. 269–86.

During, S. (ed.) (1999) *The Cultural Studies Reader* (London: Routledge).

Ebrahim, A. (2003) 'Accountability in Practice: Mechanisms for NGOs', *World Development*, vol. 31: 813–29.

Falk Moore, S. (1999) 'Changing African Land Tenure: Reflections on the Incapacities of the State', in C. Lund (ed.), *Development and Rights* (London: Frank Cass), pp. 33–49.

Fellmeth, A. (2002) '*Wiwa v. Royal Dutch Petroleum Co.*: A New Standard for the Enforcement of International Law in U.S. Courts?, *Yale Human Rights and Development Law Journal*, vol. 5: 241–54

Freynas, J. (1999) 'Legal Change in Africa: Evidence from Oil-related Litigation in Nigeria', *Journal of African Law*, vol. 43: 121–50.

Gentil, D. and J. M. Servet (2002) 'Entre "localism" et mondialisation: la microfinance comme révélateur et comme levier des changements socio-économiques', *Revue tiers monde*, vol. 43, no. 4: 737–60.

Ghai, Y. (1999) 'Rights, Markets and Globalisation: East-Asian Experience', in H. Björkman (ed.), *Human Development and Human Rights. Report of the Oslo Symposium* (Oslo: UNDP, UN Office of the High Commissioner for Human Rights/Royal Ministry of Norway), pp. 126–32.

Gilpin, R. (2001) *Global Political Economy* (Princeton, NJ: Princeton University Press).

Gomez, M. (2003) *Human Rights in Cuba, El Salvador and Nicaragua. A Sociological Perspective on Human Rights Abuse* (London: Routledge).

Gready, P. (ed.) (2004) *Fighting for Human Rights* (London: Routledge).

Hajib, N. (2000) *Human Rights and Human Development. Learning from Those Who Act*, background paper to the UNDP Human Development Report 2000, on-line at the UNDP human development report website at <hdr.undp.org>

Halder, S. (2003) 'Poverty Outreach and BRAC's Microfinance Interventions: Programme Impact and Sustainability', *IDS Bulletin*, vol. 34, no. 4: 44–53.

Hanski, R. and M. Suksi (eds) (1999) *An Introduction to the International Protection of Human Rights* (Turku: Abo Akademy University).

Hoque, S. (2004) 'Microcredit and the Reduction of Poverty in Bangladesh', *Journal of Contemporary Asia*, vol. 34: 21–32.

Hunt, P. (2003) 'Relations between the UN Committee on Economic, Social and Cultural Rights and the International Financial Institutions', in W. Van Genugten, P. Hunt and S. Mathews (eds), *World Bank, IMF and Human Rights* (Nijmegen: Wolf), pp. 139–56.

Hyden, G. and D. Venter (2001) 'Constitution-making in Africa: Political and Theoretical Challenges', in G. Hyden and D. Venter (eds), *Constitution-making and Democratisation in Africa* (Pretoria: African Institute of South Africa), pp. 1–22.

Ibhawoh, B. (2001) *Human Rights Organisations in Nigeria* (Copenhagen: Danish Centre for Human Rights).

ICHRP (International Council on Human Rights Policy) (1999) *Taking Duties Seriously* (Geneva: ICHRP).

— (2002) *Human Rights After 11 September* (Geneva: ICHRP).

Institut International des Droits de l'Homme (ed.) (2001) *Commerce mondial et protection des droits de l'homme* (Brussels: Bruylant).

Jordan, B. and F. Düvell (2002) *Irregular Migration* (Cheltenham: Edward Elgar).

Jouve, E. (ed.) (1983) *Un tribunal pour les peuples* (Paris: Berger-Levrault).

Kaul, I., P. Conceicao, K. Le Goulven and R. Mendoza (eds) (2003) *Providing Global Public Goods. Managing Globalization* (Oxford: Oxford University Press).

Khor, M. (2001) *Rethinking Globalization* (London: Zed Books).

Khor, M. and L. Li Lin (eds) (2001) *Good Practices and Innovative Experiences in the South. Volume 3: Citizen Initiatives in Social Services, Popular Education and Human Rights* (London: Zed Books).

Krishnan, J. (2003) 'The Rights of the New Untouchables: A Constitutional Analysis of HIV Jurisprudence in India', *Human Rights Quarterly*, vol. 25: 791–819.

Lake, D. (2000) 'Global Governance. A Relational Contracting Approach', in A. Prakash and J. Hart (eds), *Globalization and Governance* (London: Routledge), pp. 31–53.

Leftwich, A. (1993) 'Governance, Democracy and Development in the Third World', *Third World Quarterly*, vol. 14, no. 3: 605–24.

Lund, C. (ed.) (1999) *Development and Rights* (London: Frank Cass).

Macdonald, M. (ed.) (2003) *Transformation, Participation and Gender Justice: Feminist Challenges in a Globalised Economy* (Brussels: WIDE).

McGinnis, M. (2000) 'Rent-seeking, Redistribution, and Reform in the Governance of Global Markets', in A. Prakash and J. Hart (eds), *Globalization and Governance* (London: Routledge), pp. 54–76.

Maclean, S., F. Quadir and T. Shaw (eds) (2001) *Crises of Governance in Asia and Africa* (Aldershot: Ashgate).

Magaisa, A. T. (2003) 'Case Note: Minister of Health and Others v. Treatment Action Campaign and Others (2002)', *Journal of African Law*, vol. 47: 117–32.

Mahomed, A. (2003) 'Grootboom and Its Impact on Evictions: Rudolph and Others v. City of Cape Town', *ESR Review*, vol. 4, no. 3 <communitylawcentre.org.za/ser>

Marr, P. (2003) 'Looking Forward. Can the United States Shape a "New" Iraq?', *Miller Center Report*, vol. 19, no. 3: 6–13.

May, C. (2000) *A Global Political Economy of Intellectual Property Rights* (London: Routledge).

Merali, I. and V. Oosterveld (eds) (2001) *Giving Meaning to Economic, Social and Cultural Rights* (Philadelphia: University of Pennsylvania Press).

Meszaros, G. (2000) 'Taking the Land into Their Hands: The Landless Workers' Movement and the Brazilian State', *Journal of Law and Society*, vol. 27: 517–41.

Morawa, A. (2003) 'Vulnerability as a Concept of International Human Rights Law', *Journal of International Relations and Development*, vol. 6, no. 2: 139–55.

Muchlinski, P. T. (1999) *Multinational Enterprises and the Law* (Oxford: Blackwell).

Mutua, M. (2002) *Human Rights. A Political and Cultural Critique* (Philadelphia: University of Pennsylvania Press).

Nayyar, D. (2002a) 'Towards Global Governance' in D. Nayyar (ed.), *Governing Globalization* (Oxford: Oxford University Press), pp. 3–18.

— (2002b) 'Cross-border Movements of People', in ibid., pp. 144–73.

— (2002c) 'The Existing System and the Missing Institutions', in ibid., pp. 356–84.

Nelson, P. and E. Dorsey (2003) 'At the Nexus of Human Rights and

Development: New Methods and Strategies of Global NGOs', *World Development*, vol. 31: 2013–26.

Nowak, M. (2003) *Introduction to the International Human Rights Regime* (Leiden: Martinus Nijhoff).

Omoroghe, Y. (2002) 'The Legal Framework for Public Participation in Decision-making on Mining and Energy Development in Nigeria: Giving Voices to the Voiceless', in D. Zillman et al. (eds), *Human Rights in Natural Resource Development* (Oxford: Oxford University Press), pp. 549–87.

Oxner, S. (2003) 'The Quality of Judges', *The World Bank Legal Review*, vol. 1: 307–76.

Pallemaerts, M. and M. Dejeant-Pons (eds) (2002) *Human Rights and the Environment* (Strasbourg: Council of Europe).

Parmar, A. (2003) 'Microcredit, Empowerment and Agency: Re-evaluating the Discourse', *Canadian Journal of Development Studies*, vol. 24: 461–76.

Petras, J. and H. Veltmeyer (2001) *Globalization Unmasked* (London: Fernwood/Zed Books).

Pillay, K. (2002) 'Implementing Grootboom. Supervision Needed', *ESR Review*, vol. 3, no. 1 <communitylawcentre.org.za/ser>

Pinkney, R. (2003) *Democracy in the Third World* (London: Lynne Rienner).

Prakash, A. and J. Hart (eds) (2000) *Globalization and Governance* (London: Routledge).

Rajagopal, B. (2003) *International Law from Below* (Cambridge: Cambridge University Press).

Randeria, S. (2003) 'Between Cunning States and Unaccountable International Institutions: Social Movements and Rights of Local Communities to Common Property Resources', *WZB Discussion Paper*, No. SP IV 2003-502 (Berlin: Social Science Research Centre).

Razavi, S. (ed.) (2003) *Agrarian Change, Gender and Land Rights* (Oxford: Blackwell).

Rittich, K. (2001), 'Feminism After the State', in I. Merali and V. Oosterveld (eds), *Giving Meaning to Economic, Social and Cultural Rights* (Philadelphia: University of Pennsylvania Press), pp. 95–108.

Rodley, N. (2003) 'United Nations Human Rights Treaty Bodies and Special Procedures of the Commission on Human Rights. Complementarity or Competition?', *Human Rights Quarterly*, vol. 25: 882–908.

Rombouts, H. (2004) *Victim Organisations and the Politics of Reparation: A Case Study on Rwanda* (Antwerp: Intersentia).

Ross, J. (2004) 'Jurisdictional Aspects of International Human Rights and Humanitarian Law in the War on Terror', in F. Coomans and M. Kamminga (eds), *Extraterritorial Application of Human Rights Treaties* (Antwerp: Intersentia), pp. 9–24.

Rupert, M. (2000) *Ideologies of Globalization* (London: Routledge).

Scheinin, M. (1999) 'International Human Rights in National Law', in R. Hanski and M. Suksi (eds), *An Introduction to the International Protection of Human Rights* (Turku: Abo Akademy University), pp. 417–28.

Scott, C. (2001) 'Toward the Institutional Integration of the Core Human Rights Treaties', in I. Merali and V. Oosterveld (eds), *Giving Meaning to Economic, Social and Cultural Rights* (Philadelphia: University of Pennsylvania Press), pp. 7–38.

Seidman, A., R. Seidman and T. Walde (1999) 'Building Sound National Legal Frameworks for Development and Social Change', in A. Seidman, R. Seidman and T. Walde (eds), *Making Development Work* (The Hague: Kluwer), pp. 1–18.

Sepulveda, M. (2003) *The Nature of the Obligations Under the International Covenant on Economic, Social and Cultural Rights* (Antwerp: Intersentia).

Shelton, D. (ed.) (2000) *Commitment and Compliance. The Role of Non-binding Norms in the International Legal System* (Oxford: Oxford University Press).

Shihata, I. (1991) *The World Bank in a Changing World* (Dordrecht: M. Nijhoff).

Shiva, V. (2001) *Protect or Plunder? Understanding Intellectual Property Rights* (London: Zed Books).

Singh, J. P. (2001) 'Transnational, National or Local? Gender-based NGOs and Information Networks in India', in S. Maclean et al. (eds), *Crises of Governance in Asia and Africa* (Aldershot: Ashgate), pp. 109–28.

Sklair, L. (2002) *Globalization. Capitalism and Its Alternatives* (Oxford: Oxford University Press).

Skogly, S. (2001) *The Human Rights Obligations of the World Bank and the International Monetary Fund* (London: Cavendish).

Skogly, S. and M. Gibney (2002) 'Transnational Human Rights Obligations', *Human Rights Quarterly*, vol. 24: 781–98.

Sleap, B. (2004) '"The Most Debilitating Discrimination of All": Civil Society's Campaign for Access to Treatment for AIDS', in P. Gready (ed.), *Fighting for Human Rights* (London: Routledge), pp. 153–73.

Stark, O. (2004) 'Rethinking the Brain Drain', *World Development*, vol. 32: 15–22.

UNDP (2000) *Human Development Report 2000* (Oxford: Oxford University Press).

Van Genugten, W., P. Hunt and S. Mathews (eds) (2003) *World Bank, IMF and Human Rights* (Nijmegen: Wolf).

Vasak, K. (1972) 'Le droit international des droits de l'homme', *Revue des droits de l'homme*, vol. 51: 43–51.

Von Tigerstrom, B. (2001) 'Implementing Economic, Social and Cultural Rights: The Role of National Human Rights Institutions', in I. Merali and V. Oosterveld (eds), *Giving Meaning to Economic, Social and Cultural Rights* (Philadelphia: University of Pennsylvania Press), pp. 139–59.

Whitehead, A. and D. Tsikata (2003) 'Policy Discourses on Women's Land Rights in Sub-Saharan Africa: The Implications of the Re-return to the Customary', in S. Razavi (ed.), *Agrarian Change, Gender and Land Rights* (Oxford: Blackwell), pp. 67–112.

Wright, A. and A. Wolford (2003) *To Inherit the Earth. The Landless Movement and the Struggle for a New Brazil* (Oakland: Food First).

Zillman, D., A. Lucas and G. Pring (eds) (2002) *Human Rights in Natural Resource Development* (Oxford: Oxford University Press).

Index

Participating organizations

Both ENDS A service and advocacy organization that collaborates with environment and indigenous organizations, both in the South and in the North, with the aim of helping to create and sustain a vigilant and effective environmental movement.

Nieuwe Keizersgracht 45, 1018 VC Amsterdam, The Netherlands
tel: +31 20 623 0823 fax: +31 20 620 8049
e-mail: info@bothends.org
website: www.bothends.org

Catholic Institute for International Relations (CIIR) CIIR aims to contribute to the eradication of poverty through a programme that combines advocacy at national and international level with community-based development.

Unit 3 Canonbury Yard, 190a New North Road, London N1 7BJ, UK
tel: +44 (0)20 7354 0883 fax: +44 (0)20 7359 0017
e-mail: ciir@ciir.org
website: www.ciir.org

Corner House The Corner House is a UK-based research and solidarity group working on social and environmental justice issues in the North and South.

PO Box 3137, Station Road, Sturminster Newton, Dorset DT10 1YJ, UK
tel: +44 (0)1258 473795 fax: +44 (0)1258 473748
e-mail: cornerhouse@gn.apc.org
website: www.cornerhouse.icaap.org

Council on International and Public Affairs (CIPA) CIPA is a human rights research, education and advocacy group, with a particular focus on economic and social rights in the USA and elsewhere around the world. Emphasis in recent years has been given to resistance to corporate domination.

777 United Nations Plaza, Suite 3C, New York, NY 10017, USA
tel: +1 212 972 9877 fax: +1 212 972 9878
e-mail: cipany@igc.org
website: www.cipa-apex.org

Dag Hammarskjöld Foundation The Dag Hammarskjöld Foundation, established in 1962, organizes seminars and workshops on social, economic and cultural issues facing developing countries, with a particular focus on alternative and innovative solutions. Results are published in its journal *Development Dialogue*.

Övre Slottsgatan 2, 753 10 Uppsala, Sweden.

tel: +46 18 102772 fax: +46 18 122072
e-mail: secretariat@dhf.uu.se
website: www.dhf.uu.se

Development GAP The Development Group for Alternative Policies is a non-profit development resource organization working with popular organizations in the South and their Northern partners in support of a development that is truly sustainable and that advances social justice.

927 15th Street, NW, 4th Floor, Washington, DC 20005, USA
tel: +1 202 898 1566 Fax: +1 202 898 1612
e-mail: dgap@igc.org
website: www.developmentgap.org

Focus on the Global South Focus is dedicated to regional and global policy analysis and advocacy work. It works to strengthen the capacity of organizations of the poor and marginalized people of the South and to better analyse and understand the impacts of the globalization process on their daily lives.

c/o CUSRI, Chulalongkorn University, Bangkok 10330, Thailand
tel: +66 2 218 7363 fax: +66 2 255 9976
e-mail: admin@focusweb.org
website: www.focusweb.org

IBON IBON Foundation is a research, education, and information institution that provides publications and services on socio-economic issues as support to advocacy in the Philippines and abroad. Through its research and databank, formal and non-formal education programs, media work, and international networking, IBON aims to build the capacity of both Philippine and international organizations.

Rm. 303 SCC Bldg, 4427 Int. Old Sta. Mesa, Manila 1008 Philippines
tel: +632 7132729, +632 7132737, +632 7130912 fax: +632 7160108
e-mail: editors@ibon.org
website: www.ibon.org

Inter Pares Inter Pares, a Canadian social justice organization, has been active since 1975 in building relationships with Third World development groups and providing support for community-based development programmes. Inter Pares is also involved in education and advocacy in Canada, promoting understanding about the causes and effects of, and solutions to, poverty.

221 Laurier Avenue East, Ottawa, Ontario, K1N 6P1 Canada
tel: +1 613 563 4801 fax: +1 613 594 4704

Public Interest Research Centre PIRC is a research and campaigning group based in Delhi that seeks to serve the information needs of activists and organizations working on macro-economic issues concerning finance, trade and development.

142, Maitri Apartments, Plot No. 28, Patparganj, Delhi: 110092, India
tel: +91 11 2221081, 2432054 fax: +91 11 2224233
e-mail: kaval@nde.vsnl.net.in

Third World Network TWN is an international network of groups and individuals involved in efforts to bring about a greater articulation of the needs and rights of peoples in the Third World; a fair distribution of the world's resources; and forms of development that are ecologically sustainable and fulfil human needs. Its international secretariat is based in Penang, Malaysia.

121-s Jalan Utama, 10450 Penang, Malaysia
tel: +60 4 226 6159 fax: +60 4 226 4505
e-mail: twnet@po.jaring.my
website: www.twnside.org.sg

Third World Network–Africa TWN–Africa is engaged in research and advocacy on economic, environmental and gender issues. In relation to its current particular interest in globalization and Africa, its work focuses on trade and investment, the extractive sectors and gender and economic reform.

2 Ollenu Street, East Legon, PO Box AN19452, Accra-North, Ghana.
tel: +233 21 511189/503669/500419 fax: +233 21 511188
e-mail: twnafrica@ghana.com

World Development Movement (WDM) The World Development Movement campaigns to tackle the causes of poverty and injustice. It is a democratic membership movement that works with partners in the South to cancel unpayable debt and break the ties of IMF conditionality, for fairer trade and investment rules, and for strong international rules on multinationals.

25 Beehive Place, London SW9 7QR, UK
tel: +44 (0)20 7737 6215 fax: +44 (0)20 7274 8232
e-mail: wdm@wdm.org.uk
website: www.wdm.org.uk

The Global Issues Series

Already available in English

Walden Bello, *Deglobalization: Ideas for a New World Economy*

Robert Ali Brac de la Perrière and Franck Seuret, *Brave New Seeds: The Threat of GM Crops to Farmers*

Peggy Antrobus, *The Global Women's Movement: Origins, Issues and Strategies*

Greg Buckman, *Globalization: Tame It or Scrap It?*

Ha-Joon Chang and Ilene Grabel, *Reclaiming Development: An Alternative Economic Policy Manual*

Koen De Feyter, *Human Rights: Social Justice in the Age of the Market*

Oswaldo de Rivero, *The Myth of Development: The Non-viable Economies of the 21st Century*

Graham Dunkley, *Free Trade: Myth, Reality and Alternatives*

Joyeeta Gupta, *Our Simmering Planet: What to do about Global Warming?*

Nicholas Guyatt, *Another American Century? The United States and the World since 9.11*

Ann-Christin Sjölander Holland, *Water for Sale? Corporations against People*

Martin Khor, *Rethinking Globalization: Critical Issues and Policy Choices*

John Madeley, *Food for All: The Need for a New Agriculture*

John Madeley, *Hungry for Trade: How the Poor Pay for Free Trade*

Damien Millet and Eric Toussaint, *Who Owes Who? 50 Questions About World Debt*

A. G. Noorani, *Islam and Jihad: Prejudice versus Reality*

Riccardo Petrella, *The Water Manifesto: Arguments for a World Water Contract*

Peter Robbins, *Stolen Fruit: The Tropical Commodities Disaster*

Toby Shelley, *Oil: Politics, Poverty and the Planet*

Vandana Shiva, *Protect or Plunder? Understanding Intellectual Property Rights*

Harry Shutt, *A New Democracy: Alternatives to a Bankrupt World Order*

David Sogge, *Give and Take: What's the Matter with Foreign Aid?*

Paul Todd and Jonathan Bloch, *Global Intelligence: The World's Secret Services Today*

In preparation

Greg Buckman, *Global Trade: Past Mistakes, Future Choices*

Liz Kelly, *Violence against Women*

Alan Marshall, *Go Nuclear? Nuclear Energy -- Prospects and Dangers*

Paola Monzini, *Sex Traffic: Prostitution, Crime, and Exploitation*

Roger Moody, *Digging the Dirt: The Modern World of Global Mining*

Jonathon W. Moses: *International Migration: Globalization's Last Frontier*

Edgar Pieterse, *City Futures: Confronting the Crisis of Urban Development*

Toby Shelley, *Small is Dangerous: Nanotechnology – Prospects and Perils*

Vivien Stern, *The Making of Crime: Prisons and People in a Market Society*

For full details of this list and Zed's other subject and general catalogues, please write to: The Marketing Department, Zed Books, 7 Cynthia Street, London N1 9JF, UK or e-mail: sales@zedbooks. demon.co.uk

Visit our website at: http://www.zedbooks.co.uk

This book is also available in the following countries

Caribbean Arawak Publications, 17 Kensington Crescent, Apt 5, Kingston 5, Jamaica   tel: 876 960 7538 fax: 876 960 9219

Egypt MERIC (The Middle East Readers' Information Center), 2 Bahgat Ali Street, Tower D/Apt. 24 Zamalek, Cairo   tel: 20 2 735 3818/736 3824 fax: 20 2 736 9355

Fiji University Book Centre, University of South Pacific, Suva tel: 679 313 900 fax: 679 303 265

Ghana Readwide Books Ltd, 12 Ablade Road, Kanda Estates, Kanda, Accra   tel: 233 244 630 805 / 208 180 310

Guyana Austin's Book Services, 190 Church Street, Cummingsburg, Georgetown   tel: 592 227 7395 fax: 592 227 7396 e-mail: austins@ guyana.net.gy

Iran Book City, 743 North Hafez Avenue, 15977 Tehran   tel: 98 21 889 7875 fax: 98 21 889 7785 e-mail: bookcity@neda.net

Mauritius Editions Le Printemps, 4 Club Road, Vacoas

Mozambique Sul Sensacoes, PO Box 2242, Maputo   tel: 258 1 421974 fax: 258 1 423414

Namibia Book Den, PO Box 3469, Shop 4, Frans Indongo Gardens, Windhoek   tel: 264 61 239976 fax: 264 61 234248

Nepal Everest Media Services, GPO Box 5443, Dillibazar, Putalisadak Chowk, Kathmandu   tel: 977 1 416026 fax: 977 1 250176

Nigeria Mosuro Publishers, 52 Magazine Road, Jericho, Ibadan tel: 234 2 241 3375 fax: 234 2 241 3374

Pakistan Vanguard Books, 45 The Mall, Lahore   tel: 92 42 735 5079 fax: 92 42 735 5197

Papua New Guinea Unisearch PNG Pty Ltd, Box 320, University, National Capital District   tel: 675 326 0130 fax: 675 326 0127

Rwanda Librairie Ikirezi, PO Box 443, Kigali   tel/fax: 250 71314

Sudan The Nile Bookshop, New Extension Street 41, PO Box 8036, Khartoum tel: 249 11 463 749

Tanzania TEMA Publishing Co Ltd, PO Box 63115, Dar Es Salaam tel: 255 51 113608 fax: 255 51 110472

Uganda Aristoc Booklex Ltd, PO Box 5130, Kampala Road, Diamond Trust Building, Kampala   tel/fax: 256 41 254867

Zambia UNZA Press, PO Box 32379, Lusaka   tel: 260 1 290409 fax: 260 1 253952

Zimbabwe Weaver Press, PO Box A1922, Avondale, Harare   tel: 263 4 308330 fax: 263 4 339645